RETURN TICKET

RETURN
TICKET

BY

ANTHONY
DEANE-DRUMMOND

PHILADELPHIA AND NEW YORK

J. B. LIPPINCOTT COMPANY

1954

To

SHIRLEY

born January 13th, 1945

PREFACE

THIS IS a personal story and I needed much persuasion to write it. It is not meant to be history, but it all took place. Many of the events happened a long time ago and my memory may sometimes have played me false, but where possible I have checked the facts with published documents or with friends.

I have stated my feelings as I remember them at the time and some may consider that I have been over-hard on a few of my fellows. I hope not.

The story would not have been told at all but for help given to me in escaping by others in our party which parachuted into Italy in February 1941. All are still alive, and since the end of the war, I have seen all but one.

Ill health has recently forced "Tag" Pritchard to leave the Army, while Christopher Lea left for the Bar soon after the war. George Patterson is farming in Tanganyika, and I met Lucky running an R.A.F. mess in Malta. Only Gerry Daly and I have remained as regular soldiers.

Finally I must thank all those who gave me encouragement in writing this book. Especially Evie, my wife, who started me off and kept me at it, and Martin Lindsay, M.P., who read the original typescript and made countless helpful suggestions.

ANTHONY DEANE-DRUMMOND

Camberley

CONTENTS

MAPS

DIAGRAMS

RETURN TICKET

Chapter I

THE PLAN

"RISE AND SHINE, Pommy, breakfast's up and Portugal is on the horizon."

For a moment I could not remember where I was. It gradually dawned on me that a penetrating Australian voice was shouting that breakfast was ready, and that we had just made landfall near the northern tip of Portugal. I was on the way to Malta in a Royal Australian Air Force Sunderland flying boat, on an enterprise the like of which had never before been attempted by the British Army.

As I lay on my bunk, still only half awake, with the muffled roaring of the Sunderland's four engines pervading everything, I started to think over the last eight months. Certainly it had been the most strenuous period of my life. As athletes are trained for a race so we had been trained for battle. Four weeks' intensive physical training had been followed by real parachuting. In those days when relatively little was known about the tricks of this particular trade, we had to learn by trial and error and on the basis of our own experience. There were surprisingly few fatal accidents and there was every incentive not to repeat a mistake. All of us were volunteers coming from every conceivable unit in the British Army and nothing appeared to dampen the men's enthusiasm. So long as they thought it would bring the day

13

nearer when they would go into action, they did not mind how dangerous or exhausting their training might be.

After parachuting, we went up to Scotland to train as infantry and to be toughened up. At the end of a month of extreme physical activity which included shooting, marching, climbing, and so on, a miscellaneous collection of enthusiastic individuals had been transformed into a team, fit, efficient and, above all, terribly keen to exhibit its prowess.

The next five months were, in consequence, rather an anti-climax. We relapsed into routine training because there was nothing more useful for us to do. To us it seemed that no one knew how, or when, or where we were going to be used—and no one appeared to care. We had joined for adventure and action. After you have done it a few times the excitement of parachuting wears pretty thin, so that now all we wanted was to go anywhere and do anything to prove ourselves in battle.

Around Christmas Day 1940, six of us had our answer. We had been chosen, together with about thirty men, for an operation which was due to come off in about a month. Our excitement can be imagined, and we all congratulated ourselves on our good fortune in having been chosen for the job from the whole commando. Major T. A. G. Pritchard, M.B.E., Royal Welch Fusiliers, was to command us. "Tag" Pritchard was a regular soldier; he had got out of running a transit camp (hotel keeping he always used to call it) in order to go on active service by volunteering to parachute. In fact he was rather heavy for a parachutist, having been a good heavy-weight boxer in his younger days. In spite of a rather gruff and inarticulate manner, there could not have been a more likeable or a more loyal commanding officer. Of the remaining five officers two were demolition experts from the Royal Engineers, Captain G. F. K. Daly and 2/Lt. G. R. Patterson, a young and tireless Canadian. The protection party consisted of Captain C. G. Lea, myself, a lieutenant in Royal Signals, and 2/Lt. A. G. Jowett, our second Canadian, who prided himself on being more Scottish than the Scots, and more bloodthirsty than anyone else. At this stage we were only told enough to allow us to train efficiently—namely that we were to blow up a bridge somewhere in enemy territory.

Early in January we were joined by two Italian interpreters, Flight-Lt. Lucky of the R.A.F. and Sergeant Pichi. Both were about forty-five which is a healthy age to start parachuting. Sergeant Pichi was perhaps the most surprising member of our party—and certainly not the least courageous. In civilian life he had been banqueting manager at the Savoy Hotel. He had been interned as an alien at the beginning of the war; but, with a lot like him, he had volunteered for any job that the British Government might give him. He was fanatical, both in his hatred of the Fascists and his love of Italy. Uniform did not change him much. He was still the suave and polite little man, with a bald top to his head and a slight middle-age spread, who might be expected to be in charge of banquets at the Savoy, and no one would have recognised him as the hero he proved to be.

We all trained hard in that cold month of January 1941. We had left our comfortable billets in Knutsford, Cheshire, and had been concentrated on Ringway Airfield for the final rehearsals. In the months to come we were to look back nostalgically on the time when we had been fed and housed so well, and indeed luxuriously, by the wonderfully hospitable people of Knutsford. At that time all commandos were billeted in individual homes, the idea being that it encouraged us to look after ourselves. In fact we were looked after hand and foot by the families on whom we were billeted, and it was most pleasant while it lasted.

At Ringway we lived hard. Before breakfast each morning we went for a three-mile run, followed by thirty minutes' P.T. After breakfast we normally had a twelve to fifteen mile "parachute march." This meant covering at least eleven miles every two hours and it took some doing while carrying full equipment. The afternoon was spent rehearsing on the mock up of the bridge that had been built of wood in Tatton Park, about five miles from Ringway. It was in this park that we had done all our early parachute jumps and it was here that we carried out a complete rehearsal, including parachuting from the aircraft which we were to use on the actual operation.

Previously we had been using two or three old Mark I Whitleys, which were all the Air Ministry could spare for Churchill's newly formed Airborne Forces. The Whitley was not a very suitable aircraft from which to parachute. It was originally designed to carry a gunner half-way down the fuselage in a kind of dustbin, and when this was removed, it left a hole about four feet across through which it was possible to jump one at a time. The fuselage was about four feet high and not much wider than the hole itself, so a drill was evolved with half the parachutists sitting aft of the hole and half forward. When the pilot gave us warning over the intercom that it was fifteen minutes to the target, a scene of frenzied activity used to take place. Equipment was checked over, parachute static lines clipped to a bar above the hole, and the parachute exit doors loosened, but not opened. The doors were normally only opened five minutes before dropping, to stop the men getting frozen stiff. When the red light came on, indicating five seconds to drop, the two nearest to the hole sat on its edge facing each other, and the remaining six edged up as close as they could get. As soon as the green light came on, we dropped alternately from front and rear of the hole and it took about fifteen seconds to clear the whole "stick" of eight parachutists. The great idea was to jump as quickly as possible one on top of the other so as to land close together on the ground. One of the difficulties of "hole jumping" was to make a completely clean exit without touching the sides. If you pushed off too hard, your face encountered the far edge as you went out. If you slid out too gently, the parachute on your back bounced you off your side of the hole so that your face again met the far side! Nor did the slip-stream help, for as it acted first on the legs of the parachutist as he emerged from the aircraft, it tended to topple him over unless he went out perfectly straight. As may be imagined, there were quite a few bruised and bleeding faces walking about Knutsford and Ringway in those days, disfigured by what came to be called a "Whitley kiss." The parachute we used was of the self-opening type that required no action on the part of the parachutist. A static line was fastened between the plane and the bag containing the parachute on the man's back. Only when the parachute was pulled completely out of the bag did a weak link of thin nylon cord break and sever the parachute from the aeroplane.

At the beginning of January, eight Whitleys of the latest sort arrived commanded by Wing-Commander J. B. Tait, D.F.C., who was later to become famous for bombing the *Tirpitz*. The aircraft and crews had been specially selected and had been taken off bombing Germany, which was the Air Ministry's priority No. 1 at the time. The first job was to adapt the aircraft for parachuting, then to train the crews in the art of dropping living bombs from six or seven hundred feet, instead of live ones from ten thousand feet, and finally to carry out at least one complete rehearsal on the mock up in Tatton Park.

As we trained, so our efficiency improved and eventually we found we could place the half ton or so of explosive in position in just over half an hour. Our N.C.O.s and men could not have been better. We planned to put six parachutists, together with their arms and explosives, into each of six aircraft, leaving two aircraft spare which could be used for diversionary bombing if they proved to be serviceable on the day. In each aircraft was one officer, one sergeant or corporal, and four other ranks, whilst in containers suspended in the bomb bays, were the arms and explosives. We actually released the containers with their coloured parachutes in the middle of the "stick" of parachutists, to reduce the chances of losing all the arms and explosives. In case some failed to arrive we carried double the amount of explosive that it was estimated we would require.

My sergeant, Lawley, was a typical example of the quite excellent N.C.O.s we took with us. He had served as a regular some years before the war with the South Wales Borderers and was a trained Vickers machine-gunner. When his time expired, he became a London bus driver, which he had done for five or six years until September 1939, when he was recalled as a reservist. Born in the east end of London, he had a typical Cockney wit which he used with the greatest effect to keep up our spirits or to extract the last ounce of effort from the men when they were dog-tired.

I need hardly say that in spite of every precaution our final rehearsal did not go according to plan. A cloudy night and a strong wind combined to make the dropping inaccurate and in consequence it proved difficult and in some cases impossible for the men to collect together on the ground. About half the aircraft dropped their loads in the wrong place, so that the wretched parachutists landed in the trees along one side of Tatton Park. Those that did land correctly were dragged by their parachutes on landing, or, worse still, had to chase their arms and explosive containers which were bowling along at a brisk ten or fifteen m.p.h. over the ground. The men that had landed in the trees were unhurt, but continued to dangle in their harness unable to get down or climb up without the help of the local fire brigade, which was perhaps rather humiliating. From this minor fiasco we deduced that the operation was not feasible in a strong wind, and that though landing in a tree rarely did anyone any material harm, it was often quite impossible to get down without outside help.

At the end of the month I was told that I was going ahead to our advanced base at Malta by Sunderland flying boat and would leave immediately. I was also to act as liaison officer carrying the operation orders to the Army, Navy and Air Force chiefs at Malta, and would have to answer any questions they might want to put to me. I was then let into

the secret for the first time. We were to blow up an aqueduct in the heart of southern Italy, and then be taken off
by submarine from the west coast. The aqueduct fed the
naval ports of Bari, Brindisi and Taranto which were being
used to supply Mussolini's inglorious war in Albania and
Greece. The operation had been rather cynically given the
code name of "Colossus."

As I went over each point in turn with our planning staff,
I soon realised that our chances of blowing the bridge were
excellent, but our chances of getting away depended on
whether or not we could march the fifty miles through
mountainous enemy country to the coast.

I took the train to Plymouth where the Sunderlands were
based, and for the next seven days hung about waiting for
suitable weather. At last the met. predicted a clear patch at
about 4 a.m., and we took off from a crowded Plymouth
harbour between two air raids. I then fell asleep on my
bunk and, as I have already related, was awakened by a
cheerful Australian dishing up one of the best breakfasts I
have ever eaten. On the port side the sun was just rising
behind the Portuguese mountains and to starboard was the
endless Atlantic.

All that day we flew down the Portuguese coast and
about teatime we made a beautiful landing in Gibraltar
harbour. That night we spent merrily in a brightly-lit Gibraltar which was a strange contrast to the gloomy blackout
of England.

We took off at dawn the following day on the thousand
mile hop to Malta. The weather was glorious with the
bright Mediterranean sun shining down on the calm and
glistening sea. It made me pity all those in England which,
at that time, was shrouded in fog and snowstorms. As each

hour droned idly by, I could think of little except how the
adventure was going to turn out. Had we thought of everything? Would the pilots drop us in the right place and having blown up the bridge, how would we fare in our march
to the coast? I can remember that though I was almost
ridiculously confident we should succeed, now and again
my imagination gave me a foretaste of the excitements to
come.

When at last we sighted Malta, I remember being astounded by its brownness, and by the countless tiny little
fields into which it was divided. Even the houses appeared
to be brown and to merge into the brown-looking land. We
landed at the seaplane base of Kalafrana towards dusk,
and I was immediately whisked away to deliver up my
documents and to meet the Governor, General Dobbie.

When I met General Dobbie I was struck by his piercing
gaze, and the calm and hospitable atmosphere which surrounded him and those about him. He very kindly put me
up for the night at his house. Naturally I had only taken the
minimum on the trip and so I felt very dirty when I came
into dinner clad only in battledress, whilst all the others
were wearing starched shirts. However, they soon put me
at my ease and I had my first wartime dinner in pre-war
style. It seemed strange and very unreal to be eating a first-
class dinner in the lap of luxury when in two or three days'
time I would be living on my wits in enemy territory.

In bed that night I thought about my mother in the
Cotswolds. At that moment the news on the wireless would
just have finished and she would be going up to bed. Later
I heard that she thought that I was still training in the
north of England as a Signals officer, and had no idea that
I had been in a parachute unit for eight months. I suddenly

started laughing—what a shock she would have when she heard what I had been doing. She would hardly believe it.

On the next day there followed a frantic rush round all the various Naval, Military and Air Force H.Q.s in Malta, fixing up accommodation for the party which was due to arrive any day. The aircraft carrier *Illustrious* had been dive-bombed in Valletta harbour only about a month before and a suitable barracks which satisfied all the security requirements was exceedingly difficult to find. At length I found that the old quarantine hospital of Lazaretto, on Manuel Island, would fill the bill. It had just been taken over as a naval base and included the submarine *Triumph* which had been detailed to take us off from Italy.

When the men arrived they were highly amused by suddenly talking about mess decks and hammocks instead of mess rooms and beds. They were not so amused when they found that they had actually to sleep in them. In addition to the accommodation, which was the main worry, all the explosives and other stores that we wanted had to be drawn up, and arrangements made to transport them to the airfield. I was in Malta about forty-eight hours before the main party arrived, but those forty-eight hours seemed to pass in a flash. While I was there we had about five or six air raids, generally by single Italian aircraft which did no damage. The gun-fire sounded good and I think it was mistaken by the Maltese for bombs.

At dawn on the 9th February, 1941, all eight Whitleys arrived, much to the surprise of the R.A.F. in Malta who had expected one or two to fall by the wayside, as had always happened on previous flights to the island. They had flown the 1,400 miles from Mildenhall in Suffolk, with a fol-

lowing wind, and they arrived in record time. The officers
and men were soon seated at breakfast and then the rush
started. We had just thirty-six hours to get the planes and
troops prepared for the trip. The explosive had to be loaded
up into the containers and the containers into the planes.
Arms and ammunition had to be checked over and all rations for the operation to be dealt out. In addition, the men
had to be rested.

By 4 p.m. on the tenth, all was ready and then for the
first time "Tag" Pritchard briefed all ranks on the actual
object and the hoped-for result of our operation. Up till this
point everybody had thought we were going to go to Abys-
sinia. Maps of East Africa had been left in offices and pic-
tures of railway bridges near Addis Ababa examined. All
the troops cheered when they heard that it was going to be
Italy itself. Maps were issued and the whole plan gone
over again and again.

I may say that although the blowing up of the bridge
had been practised and rehearsed to the minutest detail,
the actual orders for getting to the coast were necessarily
vague. We were told that we would split up into several
parties and rendezvous at the same spot on the coast five
days later. Light signals were arranged for bringing the
submarine in, but routes were left to the individual parties
to work out for themselves. I don't think any of us worried
too much about this, for all we thought of was how to blow
up the bridge, and we relied on luck to get us out of the
country.

All we needed now was a favourable weather report and
we would be off. So far so good, and we all prayed that our
luck would hold.

Chapter II

THE OPERATION

The weather report was satisfactory and at about 5 p.m. we gulped down some hot tea and hard-boiled eggs. I did not feel at all hungry and as one of the men put it, "These Maltese eggs seem coated with glue." We were dressed in all our paraphernalia—over the webbing pouches we wore a loose garment called a jumping jacket and on top of that went the parachutes. Feeling very overdressed and clumsy, we took a truck to the waiting aeroplane and squeezed laboriously down the rather narrow tunnel of the Whitley. While the men settled down in unaccustomed silence, all the lights and bomb-release switches were tested. Then we heard crackling through the intercom, "N for nuts now ready to take off—over." Back came the reply, "Hallo N for nuts, O.K. Good luck. Off." We had started on our great adventure.

Our eardrums tightened as the aeroplane climbed through the sky and soon the pilot told us that we were flying at ten thousand feet over Sicily. Just over the northern coast the aeroplane started to rock and bump and we could hear the engines speed up and then slow down. This was the flak about which we had been warned, but it did not seem very alarming from the inside of a Whitley.

By now most of the men had settled down comfortably

and were nicely asleep, but it seemed quite soon when we heard the cry, "Fifteen minutes to target." Everybody was immediately electrified into action. Equipment was checked over, parachute static lines sorted out and the parachute exit doors loosened.

After what seemed a very long fifteen minutes, we were astounded to see the rear gunner come through from his perch in the tail and shout out, "You are due to drop in under a minute. Get cracking." The intercom had failed at the last minute, and for about ten seconds there was a pandemonium while we wrestled with the doors.

Suddenly I saw the light of a village flash by underneath, not a hundred feet below. I now knew that we might expect our red light in a few seconds, as the run-up to the target went straight over the middle of the village of Calitri. Sure enough, on came the red light and we all braced ourselves for the jump. We knew we had five more seconds in the plane before we started on our adventure. It seemed unreal. Why on earth was I sitting at the edge of a gaping hole looking down on Italy? Those five seconds were interminably long. I seemed to have time to think about everything. I glanced at the rest of my section, wondering what was passing through their minds. They looked cheerful but pale, and they too, were looking round at their companions. Through the hole at my feet some houses and then a river flashed by in the moonlight. It could not be long now.

"Green light!" A sudden jolt into reality. I was number five. Number six, the last one out, started counting "No. 1." "No. 2." "No. 3." "Containers." (The containers release switch was pressed and out dropped all the containers.)

The men had gone out superbly so far—and after a slight interval for the containers No. 4 opposite me dropped out and I followed.

The first thing I noticed was the silence after the incessant drone of the engines. There was a slight jerk and I found myself swinging gently a few hundred feet above the ground. I looked round to see where the rest of my "stick" were. The containers were bunched together, oscillating rhythmically under their coloured parachutes a very few yards away, and beyond them were the first four parachutes swinging like myself in the light of the full moon.

We had been dropped rather low, from not more than five hundred feet, which gave us about fifteen seconds before we touched down. I could only be about two hundred feet up at the most, and I started to take a more intelligent interest in the few square yards of Italy that I was going to land on. It seemed that I was going to drop on to a small bridge with a few cottages about a hundred and fifty yards away from it. This was our bridge. It stood out clearly, looking just as it did in the air photograph. The cottages were those that my section had to clear of all inhabitants to prevent them giving the alarm. The aqueduct was exactly as it had been described to us except that the surrounding country was far wilder and tilted at far sharper angles than we had expected. I was drifting towards the hillside just above the bridge. The ground was rushing upwards at me now and I braced myself for the landing. Just as my toes touched, I pulled on my rigging lines with all my might. Over I went on one side and the canopy of the parachute slowly lost its shape and flopped its yards of silk and rigging lines all over me. It was the best landing I had ever made.

I had come down in a ploughed field on the side of a hill about a hundred yards above the aqueduct. As I lay on the ground, I fumbled feverishly with my quick-release box, and eventually disentangled myself from the parachute and its rigging lines which seemed determined to prevent me moving off. The arms and explosive containers were only a few yards away, and these were quickly opened with the help of one or two of my section who had already joined me. I moved down to the bridge and ordered the rest of my men to divide into two parties. One was to clear some shacks just above where we had landed, and the other to clear the cottages just below the bridge which we had to destroy. I myself would be at the aqueduct and all inhabitants were to be brought to me there.

I could hardly believe that I was really in enemy Italy. The Italian countryside in the hard, clear light of the full moon looked utterly peaceful and curiously like a Scottish glen. The hills were of course much higher, some being five or six thousand feet. The chief difference was that instead of grass and heather as in Scotland, the whole country was ploughed, even up the steepest and most inaccessible slopes.

The aqueduct turned out to be much the same as the one we had practised on, with one important difference. It was made of reinforced concrete. We had expected a masonry bridge and as reinforced concrete is a far harder substance to destroy, our supplies of explosives might well prove insufficient. That, however, was a problem for the sappers to solve. While all this was going on, the buzzing of aeroplanes grew more frequent and by the flare of an occasional green Very light, we knew that further droppings were about to begin.

I was wide awake, and kept straining my eyes through the night for any signs of the rest of our party. In the original plan my plane was due to drop third at 9:42 p.m. We dropped on the tick of 9:42, but it was not until about 10:15 that there was any sign of anybody else. I remember having a rather funny feeling somewhere inside me when it occurred to me that perhaps all the other planes had lost their way and ours was the only one to arrive. I think we all had the same thought. Then we saw the parachutes idly floating down in the silent night.

There was a loud crashing through the bushes and thorn ash in the valley bottom. My men took the cue and prepared to fire, only waiting my signal in case it should be one of our own sections. But when the trees parted out came old Tag by himself, a little out of breath, as his plane load had been landed about a mile away down by the river. Carrying up all the explosives was clearly going to be hell and we decided then and there to use all the tame Italians we could find to help us. It was a funny business. We had all been prepared to kill Italians and when we arrived at the spot there were only a few peasants and they were only too willing to work for us.

By now a lot of our men were arriving at the bridge. Some were preparing to defend it, and the remainder were helping to set the charges beneath it as the Italians arrived with the boxes of explosive. The peasants told us that it would give them enough to talk about for the rest of their lives! It would be interesting to know what ac-

count of the raid is being passed from mouth to mouth at
the present time.

One of the oldest and most wizened of the peasants
suddenly exclaimed in a broad American accent:

"Are you guys English?"

Quick as a flash one of our Cockneys retorted:

"No, chum, we are Abyssinians on our way to Sunday
School."

It turned out that the old man had been a bell hop in
the Waldorf-Astoria in New York for several years, but he
had returned to his hovel in Italy as soon as he had saved
up enough money to buy his passage home.

My section was just below the bridge. Near it were the
cottages into which we had put the women and children;
Christopher Lea's was on either side of the bridge and
Geoff Jowett was opposite to me on the north side of the
stream. Our orders were to give warning of anybody coming up the valley and, if necessary, to prevent interference
with the parties carrying the explosive. There was to be
no firing unless it was unavoidable. As it happened the
only man in uniform who appeared was the local station-
master from Calitri railway station. He was duly impressed
into the labour gang and made quite a good porter, as
was only proper. His biggest worry was that he would be
late taking over from his relief and might get the sack.
If he was sacked he would be put in the army and sent
to the front, which he pointed out was far too terrible a
punishment for kind people like us to inflict on him. We told
him that his skilled labour was required, but that if he
liked we would give him a certificate to say that he had
been detained against his will. This cheered him up tre-

mendously and from then on nobody could stop him talking. He said he might even get a medal for his heroic labours. We heard later that most of these civilians were awarded medals for their brave conduct in face of the enemy.

All the time gangs of men had been passing up the track through our position, loaded with fifty-pound boxes of gun cotton. Muffled swear words streamed from their lips as they sweated. This was the only noise to be heard apart from the occasional yapping of dogs and the tinkling of a stream close by. As soon as enough explosive had been carried up to the bridge I stopped the last of the porters, who was carrying two boxes on his shoulders. It seemed such a pity to waste it so I put it under one end of a small bridge carrying the track which led to the main aqueduct. This would delay the repair work. Corporal Watson, R.E., placed the charges and I sent a message to Tag to explain what was happening and that the small bridge would be blown up as soon as I heard the big bang. The explosion of a single slab of gun cotton was the signal that the aqueduct was about to be blown up. This was to act as a warning for all the defence sections, and when they heard it everybody had to move to a safe position about two hundred yards to the west.

The sound of the warning explosion in that still air echoed and re-echoed among the hills. There was a small pause, and then we immediately started to move quickly. Corporal Watson and I stayed behind to deal with the little bridge while I ordered the rest of my section to go to the rendezvous.

Corporal Watson lit the fuse and we withdrew just behind the cottages waiting for the two explosions, the one of the aqueduct and the other from our own little bridge.

"Whoomf!" Our bridge went up in a cloud of flying concrete, iron rails and bits of masonry. I had never expected so much debris, and we were showered with blocks of concrete and bits of iron. The wretched people in the cottages set up a wail and a woman ran out of the house with a baby in her arms when the bits started thudding down on the roof. Not thirty seconds later up went the main bridge with a tremendous roar. About a third of a ton of gun cotton had been carefully slung into place against one of the piers under George Patterson's orders. The aqueduct was constructed in three piers and we had planned to blow up all three. The senior Royal Engineer officer, Captain Gerry Daly, had not arrived by the time the bridge was due to go up and we had to assume that his plane had either been lost or had failed to take off. Pat took over his duties and he decided to concentrate all the explosive on one pier. Even then, the chance that it would break was small, but it was the only hope of success, and all depended on the quality of the Italian concrete.

Corporal Watson and I went up to inspect the damage we had done to the little bridge before joining the rest of the party, who by now were all assembled about two hundred yards to the west of the aqueduct. Our bridge had been neatly cut and one end lay in the bed of the stream. We then slowly clambered up to where the rest were standing and eagerly asked for the news of the aqueduct. Tag and Pat had gone back to look at the damage and had left the rest of the men at the assembly position. Impatiently we awaited their return, all wondering what on earth we should do if there was no damage. We had been keyed up for this moment for the past six weeks and failure would have been unbearable.

Tag and Pat came back without a smile on their faces. Was it a fiasco? Tag put up his hand and everybody stopped talking. All he said was, "Listen." We all strained our ears and sure enough we heard the sound of a great waterfall. It was a success. How we cheered and cheered! We could hardly imagine that we were in enemy country. Those British cheers must have been heard a good mile or two away.

All our inward hopes and fears about the success of the venture were now soothed and the reaction made us all feel very tired. What was more tiring still was the thought of having to walk some sixty or seventy miles across the mountains to the coast.

Tag had decided before we started that we would have the best chance of getting to our coastal rendezvous if we split up into small parties and made our own way to the sea, and accordingly he divided us into three, each with about ten men and two officers. Tag and myself were with the first party, Christopher Lea and George Patterson the second and Flight-Lt. Lucky and Geoff Jowett the third.

The barks of a dog pierced the night. It seemed impossible that we would not have all Italy on our heels by the morning. We bent our backs and laboured slowly through the mud up the hills.

Chapter III

MAN HUNT

A MAN HUNT is an unpleasant thing. If you are the man
it is worse still. The bridge was blown up and we had
achieved all we had set out to do. Now came the anti-
climax; we had to get to the coast as quickly and as
secretly as possible. Tag gave orders to lighten our loads
and so all our heavier weapons, which included Bren and
tommy-guns, were taken to bits and pushed into the mud
soon after leaving the bridge. This still left each man with
a thirty-pound pack containing five days' rations, together
with his mess tin, waterbottle and a miniature primus stove.
For arms, we only retained our Colt automatic pistols, because we relied on getting to our rendezvous on the coast
unseen and unheard.

Our plan was to climb the mountain behind the aqueduct
and then follow the ridge until we reached the Sele water-
shed. From there we would make our way down the north
side of the Sele valley towards the Mediterranean. Right
from the start we met difficulties. Fields knee-deep in mud,
impassable little ravines, innumerable farmhouses all with
noisy dogs, were only a few of our obstacles. We soon learnt
to disregard the dogs, as does everybody else in Italy.
Their function in life was to yap for twenty-four hours on
end if need be. Any excuse would do, from the farmyard cat

to a sudden gust of wind rattling the kennel roof.

Every three-quarters of an hour Tag stopped and we sat down, munching chocolate or sipping a little water till we were sufficiently recovered to continue. On and on we tramped, pulling ourselves up the sides of steep little gorges by our hands and then slithering down the other side on our seats. All the jagged prominences and rocks were exaggerated by the moonlight and appeared twice their real distance away. Occasionally we had a glimpse from the tops of some of the ridges and the countryside seemed endless in its variety of obstacles, all supremely difficult for marching troops. How we cursed all Italy, the Italians and everything Italian that night!

We had left the bridge at 1:30 a.m. and we halted about 7 a.m. By that time we must have covered at least fifteen miles over the ground, but had only done six out of the sixty we had to do before reaching the coast. This meant that on future nights we would have to double our mileage if we were to get there in time.

We found a nice, sheltered little ravine in which to lie up during the day. There was a stream nearby and plenty of cover. Off came our equipment and some of us attempted to sleep before cold made it impossible. A few tried to cook some food before lying down. I had always found it best to sleep first while still warm and, when the cold wakes me, to start thinking about a meal. After a wonderful three hours' rest we were woken at 10 a.m. by the noise of a low-flying aeroplane. It was obviously looking for us and was only about five hundred feet above where we were hiding, but after ten minutes, during which we all kept our faces well down, it flew away and we did not see it again.

Miniature primus stoves were pulled out of our ruck-sacks, and after some splutters and abortive hissing, we soon had mess tins of boiling water in which we brewed sweet tea or made a greasy porridge of pemmican and biscuits. Pemmican, which is the old polar explorers' standby, is made of meat extract, with added fat, and tastes like concentrated greasy Bovril. Personally I found it quite nauseating although it may well be ideal for Arctic expeditions.

From our hiding place in the bushes we could see the Italian peasants at their work in the fields and, over on the other side of the valley, our old friend the village of Calitri perched on a small knoll half-way up the mountain. The brilliant sun and the scent of wild thyme and olive trees were all wonderful, but our hunted feeling rather prevented us from appreciating fully the countryside around us.

I shall always remember the boulders. The little ravine in which we were sheltering was filled completely with enormous boulders of all shapes and sizes. Some seemed strung together like a necklace whilst others were perched on top of one another in defiance of all the laws of gravity. Straight in front of us, not more than a quarter of a mile away, rose a sheer cliff which we would have to scale that evening. More hell to come!

Night came at last and on went our packs, with our pistols at our belts. Tag had noticed a shepherd with a flock of goats come down a path in the cliff during the day, and he said he thought he could find it. Before climbing we had to cross a small stream, not more than ten yards wide, but most unpleasant to fall into as it had deep pools and a swift current flowing between round, slippery boulders. Eventually we found a crossing place which provided stepping stones most of the way over except for a gap in the middle. Nearly all jumped it successfully, but I saw one man slip and tumble in. He had to travel the rest of that night in soaked clothes.

Tag led the way and we started to approach our cliff. When we reached its foot, we discovered that it was not so steep as had appeared from our hiding place and with a bit of difficulty we could pull ourselves up. Every bit of scrub and long grass came in handy now, and we sweated and heaved our way up the three hundred feet of mud and shingle which formed most of the surface. As we arrived at the top each man threw himself panting on the ground. It had taken every ounce of our energy to climb that hill and we felt it later on.

I was leading now and slowly we crept on in single file with ears strained for the slightest sound. We could see a few cottages against the skyline and we assumed that they must be the outskirts of Pescopegano. Dogs could be heard barking all over the village and farther up the valley. Perhaps it was one of the other parties that was causing the disturbance. I kept wondering how they were getting on.

The country looked wilder and more impossible than ever. The moonlight distorted every natural hummock and glade into grotesque and weird shapes. Before us stretched mile upon mile of the roughest country we had ever seen. Few landmarks could be picked out and so we decided to march by compass to a large crossroad near the source of the Sele river. During this night's march we had to cover some twenty miles and then to find hideouts for the following day somewhere along the north side of the Sele valley. We crossed countless small streams and stumbled through wild junipers and stunted oak thickets. We were always walking either up or down or along the side of a hill. Compass marching in this sort of country is not easy, but we managed to strike a small road which we were expecting to find.

At this stage we decided it was too risky to walk along the road, but preferred to use it as a guide, keeping it about a quarter of a mile below us. Gradually we worked our way forward, trying to avoid the scattered little farmhouses, which were becoming more numerous. At each brook we came to we first threw ourselves flat on our faces and sucked up some clear ice-cold water. Our mouths were dry with exhaustion and some of the men were completely worn out. We skirted several villages and eventually Tag decided to stop and make some sweet tea to keep us going. Soon the primus was spurting and hissing, and a welcome steam was coming off the mess tin. It was the best dixie of tea I've ever had. New energy seemed to pour into our veins as we sipped the hot sugary liquid, and when we got up a new briskness was obvious in all our party.

It was about one o'clock in the morning and as we had not seen anything on the road for some time past, Tag very wisely decided to march straight along it and damn the risk. The change of walking along that road after trudging through the mud revived us both mentally and physically. A soldier can march for miles along a road. He gets into a swing and it is only when he has to falter and stumble across country that his real weariness comes to the surface.

For five or six miles we tramped along the road and eventually we reached the big crossroad which was the highest point on our route to the coast. From now on the way ran downhill and our only task before dawn was to find a hiding place for the following day. As we scurried over the crossroad, we looked down the valley. We could see it stretching for miles in the moonlight, with rugged cultivated sides. The country looked forbidding and we could hardly believe that things would continue to go as well.

A light clopping of hooves on the road ahead startled us out of our contemplation. We were too tired and there was too little cover near the road to make a run for it and so Tag formed us into file and made Private Nastri call the step in Italian. A pony cart laden with vegetables came into view, with its big hood pulled down over a peasant woman driver. She was fast asleep and was probably taking her wares to the local village market.

The road led over the hill and away from the line of the valley, so we left it and, keeping about the same height, made our way down the side of the valley. Our route closely followed the line of the subterranean aqueduct, which at this point had been tunnelled through the hill to tap the waters on the far side. The tunnel, which is blasted through some eight miles of solid rock, is a remarkable feat of engineering.

My feet ached as they had never ached before, and my whole body was limp with exhaustion. Immediately we left the road we had to pay attention to avoid stumbling. This added to our general weariness. We continued to search for a hiding place, but nowhere suitable was to be seen. Some of us were near the end of our tether and either a hiding place had to be found soon or we would have men falling out, which was unthinkable. Our maps showed trees covering the top of a nearby hill and Tag decided to try and lie up there. We were still among ploughed fields with occasional farmhouses nestling in a fold of the valley side. As we plodded on, more and more will-power and mental energy were needed to keep us on our feet. We were drawn forward only by the fear of being discovered in those naked fields when dawn came. Thirst was again upon us, and there were no welcome streamlets in which to soak our weary faces and draw some of the cool, clear water down our dry, sore throats. We had filled our waterbottles of course, but these would be needed next day and we always kept them in reserve for real emergencies.

We climbed gradually now, hoping to strike the trees, but none could be found. Eventually we even came up to cloud level which was here below the tops of the hills. At last some trees loomed up through the mist, but when we approached we discovered to our chagrin that they sheltered a farmhouse. To have our hopes raised so high and then dashed mercilessly to the ground a moment later was no medicine for men in our condition, and we collapsed on the ground as one man. Our sweat-soaked clothes quickly became ice-cold and in the raw mist we were soon shivering from cold and exhaustion. Tag and I decided to climb up a little higher, to try to find a hiding place. We knew we could not go much farther and the men were in the same state, so it seemed the only course to take. Less than fifty yards higher up cultivation ceased, and we came upon boulders and small juniper bushes which we thought might serve as temporary hiding places. Tag went back and brought up the men and soon we had found cover of some sort to hide in. Two or three men found a tiny cave which just concealed them. It was not good, but we were unable to move another step from sheer exhaustion. We had passed the caring stage and I suppose were a little overconfident of our powers of avoiding detection.

The time was about 5:30 a.m. We had been on the move about ten hours and had covered twenty miles as the crow flies, across enemy country which had truly lived up to its name. Our feet must have travelled a good forty miles through the mud and so it was hardly surprising that we had not much energy left.

The men soon curled themselves up and fell asleep. I was not long following suit and did not wake up till dawn came an hour later. Every bone in my body ached and shivered, my clothes were still soured with sweat and my teeth would not stop chattering.

At first I could not believe my eyes but it was unfortunately too true. A peasant was standing not a hundred yards away looking intently in our direction. He had obviously spotted us and started to walk away. Tag made a quick decision and sent Pichi after him to try and convince him of our honest intentions. I knew in my heart that the game was up, but I could not believe that this was the end. We were fools to think so, but failure when we had travelled so far was unbelievable after the success that had attended our venture up till then.

Pichi came back and said he thought he had satisfied the farmer, but that there were a lot of women and children who had seen us. Some of these had gone off hot foot while he had been at the farm, to warn the local carabinieri police. He did not hold out much hope that we would get away with it. Tag decided that it was useless to try to move off as it would only attract even more attention and so we sat where we were, feeling apprehensive about what was going to happen next.

Some half naked and filthy Italian children with a few mongrel dogs were our first spectators. They sat down about a hundred yards away from us, sucking their dirty thumbs and gazing at us as if we were men from the moon. A minute or two later a peasant appeared with two pointers and a shotgun from over the hill just above our position. He seemed very frightened as he pointed his shotgun straight at Tag and kept up a running commentary, which of course was unintelligible to us. By this time quite a ring of spectators had collected, including a few peasant women who seemed to be the children's mothers. They were typical Italian peasants with nut-brown wrinkled faces, and long dirty black dresses which looked most unsuitable garments for the manual labour to which they are accustomed. Pichi was now asking the man with the shotgun what it was all about. The man then gabbled something and ended by waving his gun around to emphasise his sentences. Eventually we discovered that he wanted us to lay down our arms. As these consisted only of .32 automatics, it seemed a lot of fuss to make about singularly ineffective weapons.

The crowd surrounding our position had now become

quite large and we were rather uncertain what to do. One easy way out would have been to chuck two or three hand grenades about and then make a bolt for it. On the other hand the whole countryside seemed to be on the move towards where we were and we would not have lasted long. In addition the grenades would have killed some of the women and children, who had in the meantime been joined by more men.

I remember telling Tag that I did not agree with him when he gave the order to lay down arms.

"All right, Tony," he said, "you throw a grenade at those people on the right and I will throw mine over there."

At that moment I realised I could not do it. Women, children and unarmed peasants were everywhere and we would not be able to avoid casualties amongst them. All we could achieve were a few extra hours of freedom at the price of a particularly odious and inglorious action.

Disconsolately I agreed with Tag and he told the men. There was dead silence for a moment and then one man asked in an incredulous voice:

"Aren't we going to make a fight for it, sir?"

I had never seen such a look of anguish on anybody's face as on Tag's at that moment. He just looked at the women and then at the man who had asked the question, and said that he was sorry but that they would have to give in. Our hearts ached as we put down our pistols and told Pichi to tell the Italian that we were giving in because of the women and children. As soon as the peasants saw that we had dropped our pistols they came surging up to us and took all our equipment from us, much to our chagrin and disgust. I have never felt so ashamed before or since, that we should have surrendered to a lot of practically un-armed Italian peasants. This was the morning of February 13th, 1941.

Our farmer captors were now grinning from ear to ear with self-congratulation. Now they could truly be called the Duce's *"Eroici Truppe,"* whom they had heard so much about in the newspapers when describing some of the more inglorious moments of the Italian Army in Libya. In addition to the farmers, there were a number of creatures in army uniform who tried ineffectually to take charge and slowly we were led off to the local police, or carabinieri as they are called in Italy.

Carabinieri is a word which will recur in this story. They are a regiment in the Italian Army and combine the duties of civil and military police. The local bobby in Italy is a carabiniere as well as being the military policeman in the army. They are supposed to be specially selected and seem to be of a slightly better stamp than the average Italian soldier.

We had our first experience of these warriors just as we had breasted the rise, not more than three hundred yards from our position on the hill. A fat little *sargente di Carabinieri* led about half a dozen others. All wore navy blue serge jackets and knickerbockers of the same colour, which had a thin red stripe down the outside. They were mostly armed with an inferior type of automatic pistol which was suspended from one of the lower pockets of their jackets. Worn bandolier fashion over one shoulder was a white belt which had a small rectangular box riveted to it containing handcuffs. Their hats were of the ordinary round military type and bore the carabinieri badge of a large flam-

ing grenade. A few carried rifles in addition to the automatic. The bayonets were hinged and folded back into the
fore-end, which gave the rifle a double-barrelled appearance from any distance. The rest of the rifle was absurdly
small and light. Some British officers we met later, who
had used some captured Italian rifles, said the accuracy was
fair up to a hundred yards. Above a hundred yards even
first-class shots considered it lucky to hit a four-foot target!
This was the standard rifle in use by the Italian Army, and
could hardly have inspired confidence in the troops who
used it.

As they came up to us we could see that they were drip-
ping in sweat. When they saw us they immediately cocked
their rifles and automatics as though we were about to
attack them. Little had these people thought that war
would come to those quiet Italian villages; a "cushy" job
is the aim of nearly every Italian, and the carabinieri were
rightly annoyed that we should have been so presumptuous
as to disturb their peaceful life which up till that time had
seemed to them to be a hundred-per-cent safe.

Breathing their foul, garlicky breath into our faces they
searched us for arms, and tied us together in parties of
three or four. The Italian handcuff is made of chain and
can be tightened so that the links dig into one's flesh. Some
of us had them put on so tight that no feeling remained in
our fingers and our guards refused to loosen them. Only
Tag was spared this ignominy. Just before we started to
move again he noticed that one of our grenades had a
broken split pin. He told Nastri to tell the carabinieri this,
and also to tell them that he should throw it away—without
pulling the pin—as it was dangerous in its present condi-

tion. The flap was wonderful! The sargente began talking and shouting and waving his arms around like a side-show at a circus. He eventually drew out his revolver and, cocking it, held its muzzle right against Tag's head. His finger was on the trigger and he was trembling so violently with rage that I expected to see it go off any minute. Tag lobbed the grenade into the mud where it stuck, and may be still sitting there to this day for all I know. The commotion over, the poor little sargente, who was pouring in sweat down his unshaven face, collapsed like a pricked balloon. He looked a bit sheepish as if ashamed of his own impetuosity.

A narrow winding track led us down into the nearby village of Teora where a small crowd was out to meet us. A few shouts went up, *"Viva Carabinieri!" "Viva Duce!"* as if the carabinieri had had any part at all in our inglorious capture. We were led into the local carabinieri police station which struck damp and cold after the warm sunshine outside. The room in which they locked us up had bare whitewashed walls, and a cold red-tiled floor. Its window looked out through heavy one-inch bars on to the green hillside down which we had just come.

Chapter IV

JAIL BIRDS

AFTER BEING thoroughly searched again we began to feel the reaction to all our adventures. Food and water were asked for and eventually they appeared with hunks of bread and a few tins of Italian bully beef. These we greedily devoured and immediately felt a new energy and hope surge through our veins.

Something then happened which I will never forget. A tiny little man with a very big hat came into the room and started shouting and bellowing for all he was worth. Of course we went on munching our hunks of bread and eventually it transpired that he was a general and expected us to rise up when he entered. After a bit of hesitation Tag told us to get up, and said with a laugh that it might get us some more food if we tickled the little chap's vanity.

Sure enough he bellowed at us that we were to be treated like soldiers and heroes, and all our needs were to be attended to. The only thing he wanted to know was how many more of us there were and he received the usual answer, "I can't say." At this he just shrugged his shoulders and went out. We were to find out later that the higher ranks in the Italian Army were expected to shout even when in a small room.

Nastri and Pichi were called outside soon after the gen-

eral's departure and were questioned by a Black Shirt officer. When they came back they said that he had told them
that we were all going to be shot at dawn next day, so that
we might as well tell everything. This, of course, received
the usual laughing reply which infuriated the Italian. Italians on the whole have great difficulty in maintaining their
dignity and the one thing they cannot stand is being
laughed at.

That evening we were all pushed into a lorry and driven
to the railway station. Guards sat on all sides of us and the
men were kept chained together. We felt like a travelling
circus moving its animals from one town to the next. But
we were the animals. Hungrily we gazed at the free world
outside the lorries, with a deep, hopeless feeling inside
which increased with every minute as we sped along. The
Italians were obviously taking no chances with us, and we
never had a hope of making a dash for it.

After about half an hour we arrived at the station and
were immediately hustled into an evil-smelling waiting-
room which we were told would house us for the night.
The stench of our guards who reeked of garlic and spat
every three or four minutes on the sawdust-covered floor,
when combined with our own rank, sour smell, would have
been nauseating if we had not been so tired. Gradually we
all dozed off where we were sitting from sheer exhaustion,
and all that could be heard was a continuous heavy snoring
interspersed by the usual Italian throat-clearing followed
by a spit, a habit to which I never accustomed myself during the whole of my stay in Italy.

Morning came at last and brought with it the other two
parties which had been captured not very far from where

we had been taken. One of Geoff Jowett's party had fired a tommy-gun that he had kept, and killed an Italian officer and two peasants. When they were captured soon after, due to lack of ammunition, their clothes were ripped from them and they were rather roughly handled until they arrived at the station.

It was not until about 10 a.m. the next morning that our train came in. The men were put all together in a carriage like a dining saloon with a carabiniere in every seat near a window. The officers were split into pairs and put into ordinary six-seater compartments with four carabinieri who sat in each corner. They certainly did not mean to lose us, and we had so many guards that it was laughable. It rather flattered us that the Italians thought us such desperate characters.

We sat in the same seats all that day and eventually arrived at Naples about an hour after sunset. At the beginning of the journey our guards kept up such a monotonous series of spittings that it ceased to be a joke and Pat became so annoyed that he swore at the guards in as loud and offensive a tone as possible and pointed to the *non sputare* notice in the compartment. This terrified the poor little guards so much that a miracle happened, and the rate of spitting dropped to about one an hour. They even went out of the compartment and did it in the corridor, just to humour the mad Englishmen.

Vesuvius glowed red against the stars and we knew we had arrived at Naples. Lorries were waiting to take us to the local military detention barracks, but before the men were allowed to leave the train they were all chained together once again and taken across the station to the waiting trucks. They were outwardly very cheerful and many were the jokes dropped about the Italians and such remarks as "They say you get to like a ball and chain after the first ten years."

After a lot of talking the carabinieri eventually had us stacked in the lorries with guards on the outside all round us and ten minutes later we were herded into Naples Military Prison. The Italian version of the "glass house" is not so comfortable as in England. A high wall surrounded the prison into which a sentry box was built at each corner. The sentries were able to walk along the top of it and look down into the passage which surrounded the main prison building itself. My cell was about ten feet long and five feet broad. Along one side there was a large concrete block about two feet off the ground and about six feet long. On this was scattered a little straw, which had obviously been used before and had become damp from condensation in the cell. A very small square pane of glass high up in the end of the cell gave the only light. The door was heavily barred and bolted with a small peep hole for the sentry stationed in the corridor.

Our depression was at its lowest when we were pushed into those cells. All that night we slept by fits and starts, turning over from one hip to the other and back again. Morning came at last and with it a sentry who banged open the door and planked down a bowl of ersatz coffee with a small piece of dried fig. We heard that we were soon going to be interrogated and I think we rather looked forward to it. We were all quite confident that nothing would be got out of us, but we had heard so much about the questioning of prisoners of war that we were all curious to see what it was really like.

When the interrogator arrived he was given a room and we were all herded together in the passage outside our cells. I saw Pichi looking very depressed and tried to cheer him up. All he would say was that he was going to make a clean breast of it. "I know nobody likes the Fascists," he said. "They will soon see that I am a true lover of Italy, but at the same time a hater of the Fascist regime." It alarmed me when I heard him talking like that and I told him to keep quiet and stick to his story—that he was a Free Frenchman. I am sure he did not take my advice when he went in to be questioned and I can well imagine him telling the Fascists what he thought of them till he was led off. We never saw him again.

Two months were to go by before we read in the Italian papers that he had been shot as a traitor on Palm Sunday. We were all to feel sad at his passing. The job he had been given had been so small compared with the risks he had taken. He was a great little man.

Eventually it came to my turn, and wondering what was going to come next I went into the room. A well-dressed man in civilian clothes was seated at a desk in one corner and immediately behind him were stationed two obvious Fascists. They did not ask any questions themselves, but just stood and watched and listened. At each of the inter-rogations that I had in the next fifteen months in Italy there were always two black crows standing behind the ques-tioner.

"I am the Commandant of the camp you are going to,"

he said, "and all I want are a few details for the Red Cross."
This was a lie, of course, it was designed to put me at ease.
I then butted in on his suavity and said, "My number is
71076, my rank is lieutenant, and my name is Deane-
Drummond and you can expect nothing else." He then followed up with a few innocent questions like the address of
next-of-kin, mother's name, etc., and suddenly put a real
question. To all of these I told him, "I can't say." Eventually
he gave it up and I was sent out. Heaving a sigh of relief at
having finished something unpleasant, I went out and re-
joined Tag and Christopher who had already been through.
They told much the same story, but the questioner had used
the line that all he wanted to do was establish who was
guilty of shooting the three men. This was absurd as they
already knew the answer, and anyhow we were quite within
our rights to shoot anybody who attempted to interfere
with us, while we were getting to the coast.

Back we went to our cells and found a tolerably good
lunch waiting for us, and afterwards a shave by a barber
who had come in from the town. We felt immeasurably better now and ready to face anything. Lucky was taken off
to another part of Naples and we heard no more till the
evening. Suddenly, just after dusk we were surprised and
relieved to hear we were going to be moved to the aerodrome, where Lucky had gone already and where there
was much better accommodation and food. Up till the time
we had been questioned, the Italians believed we must be
semi-lunatics or at least criminals who had been reprieved
on the scaffold provided we jumped out of an aeroplane.
This always seemed the attitude of the average Italian.
They could never understand that we enjoyed our job. The

word *paracadutisti* always raised awe in the Italian when mentioned and we found it a disadvantage later when it came to escaping from prison camps.

On arrival at the aerodrome we were immediately hustled up the stairs of a four-storey building, and discovered that we had been allotted bedrooms on the top floor. Here were clean sheets and comfortable beds, with a wash room not far off down the corridor. I was put in a room with Geoff Jowett and we were soon fast asleep.

I woke up about 9 a.m. to find sun streaming in through the windows, which looked straight out over the aerodrome, with Vesuvius in the distance. By looking half right from our window we could see the whole of the Bay of Naples, with Capri on the skyline. It really was a heavenly room and we would have enjoyed it but for the shame of being prisoners of war.

Lunch and dinner we had together, in Tag's room. The food was sent up from the officers' mess and was plentiful and good. We were still hungry and polished off enormous plates of minestrone soup, followed by equally large dishes of macaroni, meat and vegetables. Fruit and wine were put on the table as a matter of course. During the fortnight that we were in Naples, we ate solidly and took practically no exercise, with the result that we all became very fat and spotty.

After great difficulty we succeeded in convincing the authorities that a little exercise was necessary for our health and we would be led around the aerodrome at a slow stroll by an equal number of guards. Most Italians have short legs and immediately we began to walk out to stretch our house-cramped limbs, plaintive bleats went up from the guards.

We were eventually told that unless we walked slower we would have no more walks. As a makeshift we asked to go up on to the flat roof of our building, where we paced up and down as fast as we could, trying to keep fit. The guards were all for this kind of exercise because they just sat and watched.

We asked for baths, hardly expecting them, but the C.O. of the aerodrome was a humane man and we were allowed one every other day in the officers' mess. We were taken over by guards and then had the bath. It was apparently not used much by the Italian officers as the water had to be specially heated up for us each time. On one occasion some German pilots, who had arrived in a Ju. 52 en route for Libya, were queueing up for one bath, while we were queueing up for the other. A remarkably funny situation, but we were the only people who laughed. I rather think the Germans thought that it was an Italian idea of a practical joke and were not amused.

One day we were suddenly told to get into one room as the civil *Questura* or Gestapo had come to take our fingerprints and get our photographs. Tag made a vigorous protest through Lucky and said that they had no right to do this as we were not civil prisoners, but prisoners of war. After a lot of arguing they started to take photographs, Tag scowling like a real criminal. In the middle of the proceedings the C.O. of the aerodrome arrived, and flew into a passionate rage when he discovered what was happening. The *Questura* had apparently come to our rooms direct, before seeing him and without his knowledge. He was livid. In so many words he told them that we were his prisoners and not theirs, that we were officers and what miserable worms they were. He ended up by smashing all the photographic plates that the wretched men had brought, including the unexposed ones. I have never seen anybody go away looking quite so sheepish as they did. We burst out laughing as soon as they had left and all voted the aerodrome C.O. to be several shades better than any Italian we had met up to that time.

About four days after we had arrived on the aerodrome, Gerry Daly turned up. He had stayed out five days, after being dropped about two miles north of the correct bridge. His plane had lost the way and his drop took place two hours late. He had not been on the ground more than forty minutes when he heard the two explosions from the bridges, and he had then walked to within fifteen miles of the coast and had been caught trying to get a truck. He thought that we must have all reached the beach and his only hope to get there on time was to obtain transport. Eventually he was taken to the Naples jail, from which he escaped the first night. He had noticed that the lock to his door was rotten, and sure enough it broke open to quite a small push when he tried it at about 11 p.m. With his rubber-soled boots he slipped past three sentries and wandered around Naples all that night. Eventually he found the railway with the intention of hopping on to a goods train to try and reach the submarine rendezvous. It was not until about eleven the next morning that a slow enough train came along and when he made a jump for it he somehow missed his hold and went sprawling on to the footpath. He was knocked out, and when he came to he found a soldier pointing a rifle at his head and jabbering Italian. The Naples carabinieri were the laughing-stock of all Naples when the news of Gerry's escape spread around.

Lucky was allowed to go down into Naples, under escort, to buy clothes for us, which at that time were very plentiful. I don't think Lucky realised that he was getting more freedom then than at any time afterwards when he was a prisoner. He brought back wondrous tales about the outside world, some true and some untrue. Lucky rather annoyed us at times. We had a greasy, half-shaved carabinieri officer who was in charge of our guard, and who occasionally visited us. Lucky used to kow-tow to this creature in order to get more privileges, and it sent cold shivers down our spines whenever we saw it going on. However, it did have the great advantage that we obtained a lot of concessions and generally more considerate treatment through it. By the time we were moved on to our proper camp we had accumulated quite a respectable wardrobe of washing kit and shirts, underclothes, pyjamas, etc. These we found invaluable later, and we were much better off than most of the other prisoners.

Just before we were moved, we were given a thorough search and the Italians discovered nearly everything which we had obtained before we left England. Every officer had equipped himself with some money, maps, and a compass needle. The search was quite good, but very stupidly they left a little on everybody, and when we arrived at the camp we were able to muster just about one complete set of escaping equipment, which was a great help to us later on.

We moved on the last day of February. We were told that we were going the night before and to have everything ready by 4 a.m. We packed our few clothes into

some suitcases that we had bought and at 4 a.m. we were
ushered into a string of ambulances. The carabinieri were
all dressed in their best blue and the guard consisted of
one colonel, one captain, one subaltern and thirty-five carabinieri, for the thirty-five of us. We were always considered
desperadoes by the average Italian.

The train slowly puffed its way out of Naples, after a
lot of talking and gesticulating by every railway official
in the station. We thought we were being given a special
send-off, but Lucky told us that the same sort of thing
preceded every train departure in Italy. We did not believe
him at the time but later on I was to discover how right
he was.

The track wound its way through the mountains to
Sulmona all that day. At times we were perched on the side
of precipices and at others we clattered through evil-smelling tunnels. The scenery grew wilder and more desolate
as we neared Sulmona, the birthplace of Ovid. Wide open
stretches of virgin snow, followed by nearly vertical pine-
covered hillsides, did not serve to raise our spirits. We were
all the time wondering how long we would be in the country. As each barren and deserted scene moved past the
train's windows, our depression increased, as it seemed
humanly impossible to escape from a country like this with
so many natural obstacles.

About four o'clock in the afternoon we burst out of a
tunnel and found ourselves rattling along a hillside high
above a green and beautiful valley, sparkling in the sunshine with little streams and red-roofed whitewashed farmhouses. After the desolate country we had come through
it was like looking down into a real promised land. Before

many months were out we were to hate that little valley, surrounded as it was on all sides by five-thousand-foot mountains.

By the time we had all been bundled out of the train by the carabinieri, it was obvious that all hopes of escape on the way to the prison camp were very nearly ruled out. An Italian officer from the camp who could speak English met our party. He was dressed in the olive green field service uniform of an Italian 2nd/lt. and wore an enormous pair of heavily-studded alpine boots. I wondered whether our camp was up one of the hillsides but was soon to learn that the Italian dresses more for effect than utility. He told us we had five miles to walk which cheered us up as we had not had any real exercise for the past fortnight. The carabinieri did not seem at all pleased when they heard this news and as it was starting to spit with rain they looked far more depressed than their prisoners. The Italian is accustomed to sunshine and siestas. When they discovered that our road was about six inches deep in mud, nothing could conceal their disgust. The poor old carabinieri colonel was stepping gingerly along holding his coat tails under each arm to keep them out of the mud, until about halfway when he could stand it no longer and called out to ask the Italian subaltern who led the party whether this was really necessary. The Italian, whom we soon nicknamed "Fish-Eyes" because his eyes were set very wide apart, merely grinned and said it was just as far forward as back and they might as well complete the journey. We were enjoying it hugely. It was our first exercise for the last week or two and there were some very successful efforts on the part of some of us to splash mud all over our guard.

In a way we had rather looked forward to getting to the camp. We had visions of Red Cross parcels and plenty of company from the others. We were soon to realise what a mistaken idea we all had of prison camps. On arrival we were led in through tall barbed-wire gates, and then through a door in a brick wall about ten feet high, and up a narrow passage between more high walls to a long low hut devoid of any furniture whatsoever. One end was partitioned off and one by one we were searched. Nothing was found on us and soon we were led off through a maze of walls and passages and shown our homes for the next two months. The Italians had gone to the trouble of making a small walled-off compound in the middle of the camp especially for our benefit. The officers were put in this, and the men were led off by themselves and locked up in another one which again had been specially constructed in their honour.

All the view we could see from outside the hut was the sky and a sheer mountainside. Half-way up, an old hermit's house had been built into the side of the rock, and it was the only sign of habitation that was visible from our prison. Our depression was not eased when we heard that we were not to be allowed out of our compound for any reason whatsoever. We had to feed, sleep, and exercise ourselves all in a little courtyard thirty yards long by three yards broad. It was not two days before I was down with a mild attack of jaundice, which did not help to cheer me up.

The next two months were hell. It hurt us more than most because we were used to an active life with plenty of exercise. The only saving grace was the food. At this stage of the war Italy had not yet introduced rationing, and we were able to gorge ourselves on as many eggs and as much meat as we wanted. Later on we were to know the meaning of starvation rations, but at this period we had far more than was good for us. Tag became larger every day and was reaching a colossal size when he suddenly realised it and started cutting down on his food. We soon saw that with a guard on a tower just above our yard, and also one inside all night, escape was hopeless for the time being. At first they even tried to make us keep our windows closed, but this was too much for us. As fast as the sentry tried to shut our windows from outside our hut, we opened them up again and a terrific hullabaloo started. Fish-Eyes was eventually summoned and forgot all his English in his rage. Then another Italian officer arrived who was a little more phlegmatic and reasonable and we were allowed to leave them open.

Petty annoyances of this sort continued for the whole of our stay in Italy and had the net result of making us hate and despise the Italians. This helped us in some ways when it came to trying out any particularly hare-brained scheme to escape. Anything would be better than the continual humiliation of being kept a prisoner by the Italians.

Two weary months passed before we were promoted to the top compound where all the other officers were eking out their existence. After a week or so in our first compound the atmosphere had become very strained and unnatural. We were studiously polite to each other but lack of any occupation and with not even a glimpse of the outside world except the sky above and the four walls around us, was rapidly pushing us round the bend of reason. Geoff Jowett, our Canadian backwoodsman, became more and more mopey. Gerry Daly retreated within himself and set himself mathematical problems to solve. Christopher Lea and I had pipe dreams about mad schemes to escape, but the sage old Tag ever counselled patience till we were sent to the top compound where we would at least have contact. with the outside of the camp. He was right, of course, but it was irksome to us at the time.

The American military attaché from Rome, a Colonel Fiske, visited us towards the end of our first month, and we were vociferous in our complaints of unfair and prejudicial treatment, just because we were parachutists. "You sure got the Italians scared," he said, "but I will plug Geneva Convention at them, and I reckon I will get you outa here pretty soon." He cheered us up tremendously, but the Italians could never quite rid themselves of the idea that no one could possibly want to parachute and would only do so to avoid service in Russia or a long term of imprisonment!

Chapter V

PRISONERS OF WAR

AT LAST the great day arrived and we were led up to the top compound. I remember we were held up for about twenty minutes before being let in. We grouped together and sang, "God Save the King." It sounds odd now, long after the event, but it shows how tense and worked up we must have been. Then we all trooped in through the gate feeling very self-conscious and awkward. After having seen nobody except each other for so long it really was quite extraordinary to be once more in contact with the outside world, or so it seemed to us at that time. Soon we were to tire of the company of even the hundred or so officers of our new compound and once again became more and more introspective.

Most of the prisoners had been taken in the Western Desert by the Germans and handed over to the Italians for safekeeping. One and all said how correctly they had been treated by the Germans and how disgustingly by the Italians. Like most Latin races the Italians look after everything in their power, such as animals and prisoners, in a most bullying and overbearing manner. It was their nature to push prisoners around like cattle and they saw no reason to do any differently just because we were British.

While we had been down in the bottom compound the

Italians had been strengthening the wire obstacles. They had erected three barbed-wire fences, each ten feet high, round the complete perimeter of the camp. The fences had been well constructed with taut strands of barbed wire six inches apart, the bottom strand running along ground level. Each fence was spaced four or five feet from the next, and just outside the outer one lights had been put up on the top of twelve-foot poles. These lights were ten yards apart and were kept on all night. In addition every third pole had a powerful double floodlight pointing each way along the wire. These could be switched on from the nearest sentry boxes, which were dispersed every twenty yards between the first two rows of wire. As the camp formed a rectangle about 300 yards long by 150 yards broad a guard of forty-five was required to man the sentry boxes alone.

A track for carts ran round the whole camp between the wire fences and the compound walls which were ten feet high with broken glass set in the cement along the top. Inside each compound were two carabinieri who patrolled by day and night. Still not content with what were by now most formidable defences, the Italians had erected two towers thirty or forty feet high in the middle of the camp. By day two sentries could look down on all our activities and by night they could continue with the aid of a moveable searchlight.

Such was the problem set to every would-be escaper. The over-liberal use of wire obstacles and walls, and a standing guard of fifty to sixty men on duty at any one time, made the whole camp an extremely difficult one from which to escape. Most officers said it was impossible. A few

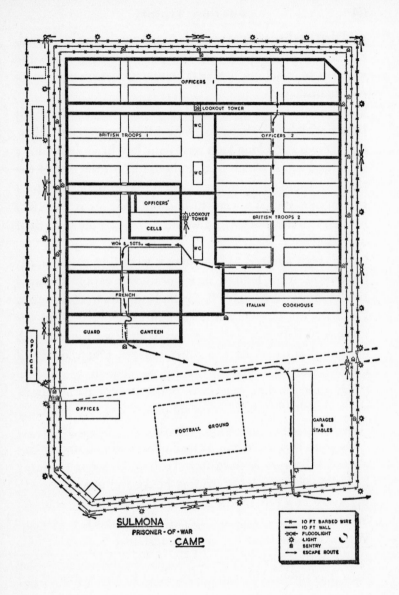

SULMONA
PRISONER · OF · WAR
CAMP

LEGEND:
- 10 FT BARBED WIRE
- 10 FT WALL
- FLOODLIGHT
- LIGHT
- SENTRY
- ESCAPE ROUTE

said that perhaps it was possible to get out, but only through a tunnel. Nearly everybody said that having got out, the chances of reaching a neutral country were a million to one against.

Our new compound was 150 yards long by 20 yards broad, which felt almost spacious after our previous quarters. Down each long side were four low brick bungalows with tiled roofs, which were to house us for the rest of the time we spent in Sulmona. A wide gravel path ran down the middle, and we were to find out that six round trips to each end and back again would give us a mile's worth of exercise.

We were allotted to bungalows according to our rank. Subalterns were housed in a dormitory, captains shared small rooms, whilst field officers had cubicles to themselves. Geoff Jowett, George Patterson and I shambled off to our dormitory carrying our suitcases which were eyed with envy and surprise by the other officers. Our room held twenty, and I was given a bed by the door. In the middle stood a red earthenware stove with the pipe going out of the wall. The floor had the usual chequered red and white tiles, which in winter were horribly dank and cold.

By each bed there was a small cupboard and one or two chests of drawers were scattered round the room. On some beds officers were lying reading books and one was working away at a table with a pile of heavy-looking volumes in front of him. Our guide turned out to be Lt. R. Ross of West Australia, and he had the next bed to mine. Short, stocky and of a swarthy appearance, he looked more Greek than Australian. He was a wonderful teller of stories and he would ramble on for hours about his past loves and adventures.

Soon after arrival, we were summoned to meet the Senior British Officer who was an Australian lieutenant-colonel. Short and grizzly, with close-cropped grey hair, he squinted at us through his glasses with obvious disfavour.

"I want you to realise," he said in a high-pitched twang, "that I have had very great difficulty getting the Italians to give us the few privileges we have. The Commandant tells me that you are very dangerous prisoners and he hopes I can control you. I do hope you will co-operate with me and help us keep our few comforts."

He was the only Australian I ever met who was not an ace fighter, so he provided the exception to prove the rule. Bob Ross was quite apologetic about him when we came back. We must have looked very gloomy and bewildered.

"Senior British Officer, my muckin' oath. Son of a Bitch or S. O. B. for short we call him," explained Bob.

Tony Rowley, another Australian, chimed in:

"S. O. B. giving you his old woman pep talk, I suppose."

"He told us to be good boys."

"Take no muckin' notice, cobber. The old man sweated out all his guts in New Guinea before this goddamn' muckin' war, and now he has none left."

Tony Rowley was in typical dress. Crumpled open-neck khaki shirt, khaki shorts and leather sandals, he looked sunburnt and healthy. With a shock of fair hair and a wide open grin, which displayed two or three badly chipped teeth, he accepted you at your face value "and no muckin' about" as he called it. He had left school at the age of seventeen to go and fight as a mercenary in China against the Japanese. By the time war broke out in September 1939, he had already served three years in Chiang Kai-shek's army and was earning £100 a month.

"Good muckin' war that was," he said. "Paid in advance and a bonus for patrols and anything dangerous. 'Course you 'ad to look out for yerself. My bank in Sydney 'ad to wire me each month that the pay was in before I would budge an inch on the First. Soon as war broke out in '39 I packed it in, of course, but wish I 'adn't now. Gave me £500 bonus, the old bastards did. Good paymasters, the Chinese."

A bell clanged, and a cry of "Lunch up" came from outside. We drifted off to the mess room and, arming ourselves with a couple of plates, were doled out our meal at the door to the kitchen. Food was still good and plentiful and was chiefly limited by what a 2nd/lt. could afford to pay. No rations were issued free and several Italian officers were employed full time to do our buying for us in the town and to keep our accounts. A 2nd/lt. was credited 750 lire a month, a lieutenant 950 and so on. This meant that the maximum messing charge that could be levied and still leave the wretched 2nd/lt. with some pocket money, was about 600 lire a month. The most iniquitous part of the whole scheme was that the equivalent in sterling at the rate of 72 lire to the £, was deducted from our accounts at home. A junior prisoner in Italy did not save any money as a result. It also meant that the more senior officer had a great deal of surplus cash, with which he could buy extra food and clothing. At this early date we had so much that it did not matter. Later on, in September 1941, when Italy suddenly enforced very strict rationing, it was to cause many bitter feelings. All non-rationed foods became fantastically expensive and the senior officers were the only ones able to afford the prices.

The number of officers who really wanted to escape from Sulmona was very small indeed. A minority said quite openly they did not want to escape, they saw no point in it and if ever a tunnel was built and if they were ordered to get out through it, they would start building another one now, through which to get back inside the camp again. One great oaf over six feet tall, with size fourteen shoes and who continually boasted about his pre-war membership of Lloyds, said this, and that he could not see any point in exerting himself or endangering his body, and was quite content to while away the time until the end of the war. He was honest enough to admit it and there were many who felt exactly the same, but did not talk so openly.

The average officer would make an attempt to escape if given a really safe way out through a tunnel or some other means, but did not have the imagination or the guts to get on with it by himself. Secretly in his own heart his mind had been numbed by being taken prisoner, and he no longer had the power to make himself take risks against what he liked to regard as his better judgment. Some were married and uttered the age-old cry of, "But I have to think of my wife and children"; others said they were engaged; others had neither the brains nor the imagination, both of which are essential to a successful escape, to do anything except follow in somebody else's lead. If you really wanted to be openly disliked by about twenty-five per cent of the officers and secretly disliked by another fifty per cent, it was to announce that you were actually making plans to escape. "Oh, but think of all the privileges we shall lose when they discover your escape," they would say. "And anyhow once you have got out of this place, which is obviously impossible, it is equally ridiculous to expect anybody not talking good Italian and dressed in perfect civilian clothes, to reach the Swiss frontier, which is over six hundred miles away by road."

Those of us that were keen to get away set the pace for the rest. Lt. Michael Pope, R.N., had been caught after the submarine *Oswald* was rammed in the Messina Strait. A nicer chap was difficult to imagine. He and Flight-Lt. Garrard-Cole had escaped from Sulmona about three months before we arrived, and had walked over the mountains through deep snow to the coast hoping to get a boat to Jugoslavia. A coastguard patrol had picked them up just when a likely boat was being looked over, and that ended the first real escape from Sulmona. After this the sentries were doubled and all the outside wire was put up, the lighting improved and in the end the impregnability or rather the inescapability of Sulmona became a byword in Italy.

Shortly after arriving in the top compound, all six of us feverishly looked around to find a way out, causing not a little amusement to the rest of the camp and not a little chagrin to some. A tunnel was projected and was soon under way. A piece of cracked concrete served as the opening and the entrance and cover were prepared. The big mistake with this attempt was the number of officers employed on it. Some twenty were digging and scattering the soil and at least another twenty were in positions round about watching for the approach of any of the carabinieri guard.

After my brief experience of tunnelling in an eighteen-inch square hole, I will vote the maximum increase to any miner that cares to strike for more wages. The entrance gave on to a fifteen-foot shaft lined and revetted with fire-wood to stop the loose sand crumbling and filling in the tunnel. From the initial shaft a tunnel went straight under the wire, a good forty yards away, and would then have to continue at least another thirty yards before it would be safe to strike upwards. Six weeks of hard work went into it with the usual tunnellers' method of scattering earth everywhere in thin streams from pockets. If one saw a collection of officers shambling around, hands in pockets, one knew that a steady stream of sandy earth was coming out of sacks held inside their trousers like hourglasses running out. The level of ground in the officers' compound must have been appreciably raised over the years that would-be tunnellers steadily scattered literally tons of earth evenly over the whole area. But tunnels in this camp were doomed to failure, especially when large numbers were employed on making them. Somehow the news always leaked out and sooner or later the other ranks' compound heard of it. As soon as this happened the Italians seemed to know. There was at least one informer among the other ranks and I don't believe he was ever caught out. One day a party of carabinieri came in and walked straight to the tunnel entrance and dug it up. All our labours of the last six to eight weeks had been in vain, and one more tunnel proved to be an abortive effort.

Ever since this occasion I decided that if ever I should escape it would be a solo or at most, a dual effort, and then there would be no chance of anybody else getting to hear of it. Many said that it was not feasible to go many hundreds of miles in enemy territory alone. I always felt that alone I would only have myself to worry about and, given self-confidence and a lot of luck, that there were good chances of success. My later experiences proved to me that I was right. Since then I have talked to several other successful escapers and they have all agreed with me that very few complete parties were ever successful, and nearly all those that got away arrived in a neutral country by themselves. This perhaps does not apply to the evading type of escape so common during the Second World War, when pilots who had never been made prisoners of war walked through occupied countries in large groups. In these cases they were aided by a complete underground organisation and it was probably more convenient to move evaders in batches; but this would never have worked in Italy before the Italian Armistice in September 1943, or in Germany.

My first idea on a way out came to me while watching the garbage being wheeled out in barrows and dumped just outside the wire. The snag was that the Italian form of wheelbarrow was very small and the garbage was carefully scrutinised by the guards. But I thought that if a very large sack of vegetable peelings went out every day as a matter of course, then one day when all suspicions had been quietened, I would substitute myself for the vegetable peelings. All went well during the next three weeks. I had to take into my confidence one of our batmen who did the wheeling out, so that he would not be surprised at an extra heavy sack. Two days later, the day before my D-day, the guards suddenly started searching every sack and even pushing bayonets into every barrow load. My first serious effort to get away had been thwarted by too many people knowing about it and once again impressed on me the need for complete and absolute secrecy when making plans. I had a long talk to the chap in whom I had confided, and eventually he admitted that he had bragged about it to a pal in the other ranks' compound.

Chapter VI

SULMONA MEMORIES

DURING THAT long summer and autumn of 1941 some of us were very depressed by the distorted war news as put over by Fascist Italy. The Russians withdrew hundreds of miles at a time and the annual circular tour from Egypt to El Agheila and back seemed to show precious few rays of sunlight in a cloud-darkened sky. About once a week we were taken out for walks around the local countryside and I enjoyed these more than anything else. The pace was slow because of the grumbles from our little Italian guards who sweated along on all sides. Sometimes we walked up the mountain at our back and had a beautiful view over our valley. Pine trees grew on every patch of soil, and thousand-foot cliffs stuck out like sentinels over our heads. Up one cliff was perched a monastery which held an old hermit, who could occasionally be seen begging for alms in the local villages. In the evenings we had games of basket ball on our only level piece of ground which was big enough, and teams worked fast and furious as did old Pop Sharpe, an Australian bookmaker, who ran a book at one side and made small paper fortunes on the result of the game. Eventually we had to stop playing because it wore out our boots which had become difficult to repair or replace.

There was no food rationing in Italy until the autumn of 1941, when they suddenly realised that the war was not going to be won by Mussolini talking from his favourite balcony in Rome. When rationing was applied the scales were far smaller than at any time in England, and the wretched prisoners were made to stick to them and had no access to the black market as did ninety-nine per cent of all Italy. Another result of having no rationing in Italy early in 1941 was the almost complete absence of Red Cross parcels. The individual officer or man thought himself lucky if he received one parcel a month. During the fifteen months I was a prisoner in Italy I received only twelve parcels and for about half this period we were on real starvation diets. I believe the situation improved later on, but I know that the early winter of 1941/42 at Sulmona was a very lean time. Well do I remember saving the crumbs from my daily ration of two hundred grams of bread so that a bread pudding mixture could be cooked up for a *bonne bouche* on the following Sunday. The thought of the next meal was ever present in our minds and the issue of Red Cross parcels was a real red-letter day, if you were lucky enough to get one. I really think that if the Italians had chucked a few buns into our compound we would have rushed for them like a pack of half-starved dogs.

It was not surprising that under these conditions all the worst in human nature came to the surface. Perhaps I have been too hard in describing what most officers thought about escaping, for their attitude may well have been the natural one. A semi-starvation diet, combined with the boredom of prison life, was bound to produce those unchristian vices and jealousies that civilisation tends to keep beneath the surface in a world of plenty. All those who served their time as prisoners of war agree that most people's natures were bared to the bone, and quite a number did not show up well because of it.

The usual classes in every subject were run from Big Business by Victor Seely to Farming by Nigel Strutt. Every language could be learnt and a few studied law. I myself tried to learn German and Italian as I thought both might help my escape. During my German studies I translated a complete German textbook on Gliding by the German expert Wolf Hirth. Gliding and soaring had been my peacetime hobby, and long were my daydreams while I cast my mind back to those pleasant summer days riding on silent wings above the English countryside. The translation of the book taught me German and gave me plenty of food for thought of a type far removed from my surroundings. It helped me keep my mental balance during those long days in captivity. There were a few officers who could find nothing to do, and they became decidedly queer. They got overwhelmingly depressed and enormous self-pity welled up within them to produce a rather pitiable creature that unfortunately was destined to become more and more common as the war years went by.

So went the prison routine. Sleep, breakfast, roll-call, work on a language or do a mile or two up and down, listen to a lecture by some expert on an unusual subject, lunch and so on. Week in, week out. Boredom mixed up with an eternal longing for freedom. Occasional "black days" when everything seemed futile and a waste of time, and even more occasional rosy ones when an innate optimism strove to show that there must be a silver lining somewhere.

Although we were completely encaged behind wire, most of us learnt quite a lot about Italy. Our guards were typical Italian peasants, who on occasions would drop remarks which showed that they too were sick of guarding us and wished only to be back in their own home valleys. We read the Italian papers which were stuffed full of propaganda to bolster up a flagging Italian morale, but in so doing revealed their weaknesses to us. Our walks took us through many small villages or past ramshackle farms whose buildings were typical all over Italy. The rough cottages were of the usual Italian peasant type, horses and livestock on the ground floor with the sleeping rooms directly above them. The roof tiles were laid on in a very haphazard way and showed many gaps to let in the weather. The life of these peasants was continuous toil by day, with a little vegetable soup and a comparatively large amount of bread to eat in the evening. Macaroni or *pasta* was a very exceptional luxury. Clad only in the barest minimum for warmth, all sexes and ages dug, sowed and reaped their fields by the unaided sweat of their own bodies. Ploughs and mechanical aids to farming were of no avail in these mountains. The only method of cultivation was hand digging, hand sowing, hand hoeing and hand reaping. No wonder the Italian family is a large one. The more sons and daughters the farmer could get to work, the bigger the acreage and the richer he became.

Bob Ross told many a story about the Italian immigrants to Queensland to farm sugar cane. On arrival they immediately went to work and saved every penny for the day when they could return to their home village in Italy.

"Italians are no muckin' good as immigrants," he would say. "Work far too muckin' hard for a dinkum Aussie. Never got drunk. Never spent their pay. Just lived in a tin shack and tried to buy good Aussie land. Sometimes we got mad and ran them right outa town. Our Italians looked pretty slippy come pay nights when we got drunk."

The tale of the returning Italian to his home town after forty years in a foreign country is a very common success story in Italy. There seems to be a strong homing instinct in them and although they could have settled in their new found countries and enjoyed a high standard of living, most preferred to return to their hovel birthplace in Italy. It is no love of Italy as a whole that brings them back, but love of one town in Italy, and one family. To have made good overseas, and then return, is a very high honour, which will place him above all his fellows at home. There are, of course, other attractions. The life led by an Italian peasant is almost medieval in its simplicity and freedom from cares and worries. If the harvest is good they have plenty to eat for the next year or two. In wartime, of course, it was all different. Only the aged and infirm were on the land and many were the complaints we heard about the removal of the workers in the family just at the time when the old ones felt that it was their turn to sit back and rest from the heaviest labour on the farm.

Sometimes we had a party in the evening. Somebody would say that he had a birthday, or that his mother-in-law had died, or that Wavell had passed Benghazi; any excuse would do. We subalterns could not afford to drink much, as most of our pay was going on extra food, but just occasionally we saved up enough vino and sitting round the red-tiled stove would tell nostalgic stories or sing lewd songs. Bob Ross had an inexhaustible supply of filthy ballads, which he would croon away to his own accompaniment on a banjo. The red acid wine would be warmed in the prisoner's own tin mug or mess tin and slowly sipped down. Somebody had a brilliant idea one week and stored all the wine for a party in an enamelled pail. Only when we started to ladle it out did we see that it had dissolved the enamel and we now had an iron bucket with an enamel rim. We drank it all the same. I do not remember that I had any worse a headache than on previous occasions.

Naturally we kept worrying the Italians to give us more privileges, take us on longer walks, buy us more things from the shops and generally see what we could get out of them. Anything important we raised officially through the Senior British Officer who had to go and see the Italian Colonnello, who commanded the camp. For smaller things we nagged at the Italian interpreters, who were mostly quite helpful, but they nearly always returned with the story that it was not possible. "If you would only all sign an undertaking that you would not try to escape, we could do much more for you," they said. "We know that your army says that it is your duty to try, but surely you can see it is quite impossible and it would save us all this unpleasantness. Of course, we know why you want to escape, and we sympathise deeply."

"Oh, really, what is the reason, then?"

"Women, beautiful women. We don't understand why you don't all go crazy. We would give you some women from the bordello, but we don't think your authorities would do the same for our prisoners in England. Still, we know where to look if you do get out."

We heard later that the camp standing orders laid down a procedure in the event of an escape, included in which were instructions to ring up all brothels within ten miles.

I, myself, was not seriously worried by lack of feminine company after the first month or two. Civilisation seemed so far away, and our life and thoughts so introspective and self-contained that sex became a very unimportant subject. It was no good longing for the company of women, there just were not any. We were not in a position to covet our neighbour's wife; he had not got one with him.

Every night the two prowlers in each compound used to make a spot-check on one or two of the dormitories to see if all the beds were occupied. After 11 p.m. we had to be in our correct rooms and if caught elsewhere we would be awarded an automatic seven days in the cooler. One night a vino party went on longer than usual and left three very merry officers drinking in one corner, when the carabinieri were heard entering the hut. Two of the three should have been in another room and one took a flying leap out of the window and was back in his own bed before the guards knew what was happening. The other one decided to hop into the nearest bed and dived under the bedclothes to the consternation of the occupant who had gone to sleep two hours before.

The guards must have suspected something because they stripped back the bedclothes and were highly amused to catch two officers in one bed.

"We now know how the English take care of their feelings. We always thought something like this must be going on, and now we have the proof."

The incident gave us a good laugh, both at our two and the Italians.

When we came up to the top compound we discovered to our surprise that no attempt had been made to organise or help escapers or to centralise the camp's slender resources of escapers' equipment such as money and maps. Those that were keen to escape were few in number and rather resented the idea of being told what to do by a committee of senior officers for whom they had little respect.

Tag immediately set himself the task of setting up some sort of escape organisation and of convincing everybody that it was a good thing. Using a great deal of tact and gentle persuasion, he eventually won over even the oldest of the camp's inhabitants, many of whom had acquired invaluable adjuncts to escaping such as wire-cutters, compasses, maps, lire and even civilian clothes. Major S. Clayton, D.S.O., of the Long Range Desert Group, soon became an expert forger of documents. Lucky extracted railway timetables from the Colonnello's office whilst acting as a spare interpreter. Information was obtained on the conditions at the frontier, and many other data and facts assembled for the use of anybody who could surmount the first and worst hurdle, of actually getting out of the camp itself.

Any officer who thought he had an idea on how to escape was to register his scheme with the organisation, to prevent two rival parties attempting the same method unbeknown to each other. If approval was given, then sufficient of the camp's resources would be allocated to ensure the maximum chance of success. To preserve secrecy we did not know who formed the whole organisation, but only our own representative on it. Naturally Tag was ours, and I am sure he was the leading spirit who inspired the whole thing.

The one source of inspiration for me and a few others was the idea of making a successful escape to a neutral country. To some the only object was to get out of the camp and have a good walk around and taste some freedom from the horrible camp routine. To me this was not half enough, and I could see little point in getting out if a sound plan did not exist to get to a neutral country. The mere fact that everybody in Sulmona said that it was impossible to make the six hundred mile journey to the Swiss frontier was an added incentive to prove the know-alls wrong.

Chapter VII

PLANNING FOR FREEDOM

THE SUMMER passed and still we had made no serious
attempt to get out. Prison routine was beginning to
numb our senses and like the older inhabitants we had
half convinced ourselves that it was impossible to escape
from Sulmona.

It was Christopher Lea who broke the spell. One morning, when we were striding up and down the compound,
he said:

"You know, Tony, it is high time we made some effort to
get out. It is all very well to say it is well-nigh impossible,
but there must be a way out somewhere."

"I only wish I could see one."

"Well, what about putting a ladder against the wire in
the corner and just running across."

"You have two sentries within a few yards and they
would have plenty of time to shoot at you."

"They might miss."

"Not at ten yards. No, Christopher, we must do better
than that. We must have at least a fifty per cent chance of
getting out undetected."

"We just must do something."

"All right. Let us do it methodically. We must examine
every inch of the whole perimeter wire and see if there is

anywhere which is less well covered by sentries or where the wire is not continuous."

"That's right. And having found the weak spot we must then work out a way of getting there from our compound. Come on, let's draw a plan of the outside wire and check it off as we get a chance of looking at it."

The best opportunity we had of inspecting the outside wire was when we were taken for walks. We were then led out of our compound and round the outside walls till we reached the sentries by the main entrance gate. Four or five weeks elapsed before either one or other of us saw the place we were to use some six weeks later. It was right down at the bottom end of the camp where the ground level changed at a wall. The three rows of wire ended there and then were started again at the top, but about ten feet higher up. The end poles of the three fences were spaced back from the edge of the wall by about eight inches to allow the poles to be stayed by wires running at an angle. Apart from these stay wires, the ledge was free of obstruction and led to freedom.

We had found a gap in the wire which had seemed so impregnable, but there were many snags. In the first place a sentry box was placed about fifteen yards away on the lower level. Secondly a light shone continuously on the gap from the wall of the stable and kept the whole ledge lit up. Thirdly the gap we had found was at the diametrically opposite end of the camp to where we were. To any but us poor caged birds the problems would have seemed insurmountable, but we had now been prisoners nine months in the hands of our despised Italian captors, and we were willing to take any reasonable risks. It took us a month to work out a plan between the two of us. First I would have a bright idea and then Christopher would have a better one, and each of us spent all day and every day with our minds concentrated on this one problem.

We first of all decided that, provided the night was dark enough, we could get out along the ledge if the light was put out. This was the crucial point on which the success or failure of the whole plan turned. A really wet night with no moon behind the clouds would have suited us admirably. One of the first problems we came up against was how to turn out the light. We thought of everything. We could fuse the whole camp supply, but turned this down because it would alert all the guards and the fuse might be repaired before we could get to the right place. Anyhow it turned out that the perimeter lights were on a separate circuit from our own.

Our next idea was to bribe the Italian electrician. However, at this time our guards appeared to be singularly incorruptible and we thought we might easily be double-crossed. Only a few weeks before, one of the officers had tried to bribe a guard who immediately told his officer about it. He was allowed to keep the bribe and was promoted lance-corporal! It turned out that this was a standard rule in Italy at this time and was instigated by Mussolini in an attempt to eliminate corruption among his Italians.

Our next idea was to wait for a thunderstorm and hope that the lights would go out. Power systems in Italy did not seem as efficient as in Britain and nearly always broke down in heavy rain. We rejected this scheme because it gave the initiative to the weather, a most unreliable factor.

Eventually I had a brainwave whilst sitting in the lavatory (surely a great stimulant to intensive thought the whole world over). We would carry a ladder to the light and, pretending we were Italian electricians, would climb up the ladder and unscrew the bulb. It all seemed so simple once we had thought of it. So often it is the obvious that eludes one.

There were difficulties of course, not the least being the manufacture of the ladder and getting out over the compound walls to start our walk to the light. Italian uniforms would have to be made and worn over our escaping clothes, which we were busy collecting together in the meanwhile. Tag gave me a civilian-looking raincoat, which he had persuaded the Italians to buy for him while we were in Naples. The biggest problems were the hat, trousers and shoes. To get the material for the trousers, I induced the Italian lieutenant who did some shopping for us, that some really strong cloth was required for a home-made deck chair that I had constructed. He came back with two yards of dark green corduroy which was ideal for my purpose and I set to work with needle and thread to sew them into some semblance of trousers. They were shaped on the model of battledress trousers but unfortunately I made them far too tight across the seat which was to have repercussions, or rather rendings, later on.

Our last serious hurdle was how to transport ourselves and our ladder, once made, outside the compound walls without exciting suspicion. This problem alone might have floored us, but we had so nearly found the solution that there would have to be an answer to this one. The top three sides of the camp had sentries facing the outer walls and only a few paces from it. We could never have dropped over that wall with a twelve-foot ladder and got away with it. The only place where the sentries were away from the outer wall was in the bottom end of the camp and next to the French compound.

Yet another difficulty cropped up: could we trust the French not to raise the alarm if they saw us passing through? Eventually a reliable Frenchman called Pierre was vouched for by Sergeant Clements who was one of our own N.C.O.s. We, of course, would not tell Pierre a word of our plans, but on the chosen night Clements would get hold of him and he would keep the rest quiet while we went through. At the bottom of the French compound was a narrow passage between their boundary wall and the guard room. There was no sentry in this passage and a corridor led right through the guard room from one side to the other and connected the passage to the outside. All we had to do was to drop over the wall at the bottom end of the French compound into the passage, and then to march boldly through the corridor and out the other side. There was a sentry outside the door, but he would be looking outwards and he certainly would not expect prisoners to come out of his own guard room carrying ladders! We would then walk with our ladder straight to the lamp-post and proceed as before.

It was about the end of November that we heard that Donald Stuart had reached Switzerland to make history with the first successful escape from an Italian prison camp. Gradually the details leaked out. He had pretended he was sick with some kidney trouble at Sulmona and had been sent to Chieti hospital only five miles from Pescara on the Adriatic coast. Donald Stuart's job in peacetime had been with the Suez Canal Company and he could speak French and Italian like a native. He also looked like a Latin. With these advantages he would have a very good chance of getting out and to our glee we heard he had been successful. Travelling as a civilian on the trains all the way to Como, he crossed the frontier without much difficulty near Chiasso. I heard later that he spent one day bathing in Lake Como and even had his photograph taken on the beach giving a fictitious address in Milan. News of this success encouraged us, and reassured me that it was possible to get to Switzerland no matter who said the opposite.

All we had to do now was to make a twelve-foot ladder and transport it down to our starting point in the N.C.O.s' compound. Ladders do not grow on trees in prison camps, but compared with our other problems this required but little thought. A loose plank was soon split down the middle, to make the two shafts and pieces of firewood and chairs made the rungs. We decided it would be easiest to take the ladder down in pieces to the N.C.O.s' compound two nights before the attempt, and for our N.C.O.s to assemble it down there. They had an excellent hiding place under some rafters and were confident that they could conceal the sound of hammering with a lot of table beating and singing. Those two excellent N.C.O.s of ours, Sergeants Lawley and Clements, offered to do the whole transportation and assembly and we let them carry on. They came up to our compound, fetched the bits and pieces, and took them down to their compound over two of the intervening walls and practically under the very eyes of the "Crows" patrolling in the compounds. They would wait until they were looking the other way or round one corner of a building to

rush the pieces of wood another fifty yards on their way.
As the searchlight's beam from the tower swung round, it
would find them and their load motionless in some shadow.
Sergeants Lawley and Clements completed this operation
with a hundred per cent success, and the ladder was assembled in the next few days in the N.C.O.s' compound
without any suspicions being roused on the part of the
Italians.

We were ready for our big adventure. It was December 4th, 1941 and we had been in the bag for nearly ten
months. We were tremendously excited at the prospect of
being able to do something at long last. It had been full
moon on December 2nd, so that by about the seventh or
eighth we would have the first half of the night with no
moon at all. The year was getting late but the weather was
still tolerably fine. Soon we would come up against the bad
weather, likely in January, and we decided, rightly or
wrongly, not to wait for a wet night but to make our first
attempt on the night of December 7th.

Christopher and I disagreed violently on the best method
to use once out of the camp. Mine was to walk the fifty-
odd miles to Pescara and buy a ticket on a train from there.
His plan was to hop goods trains all the way up Italy. Mine
was certainly the quicker and more spectacular, but Christopher thought that it had little chance of success. He did
not think that an Englishman with fair hair could go into
a southern Italian railway station and buy a ticket hardly
knowing a word of Italian and get away with it. It was too
fantastic for both Christopher and the members of the committee to whom we related our detailed plans to get away.
But I insisted that booking-office clerks have a difficult

time, and all they wanted to hear was "Third single London" or "Milan" to push over a ticket automatically. I learnt and relearnt the phrase asking for a ticket to Milan. "*Terzo Milano*" became my sleeping song and my pronunciation was said to be perfect by our tame linguist, old Lucky. My idea was always to make for large towns, and to mingle with people and queues where possible. Safety in numbers would be my motto. I also relied on walking to Pescara in three nights. The first night I would go straight up the Majella Mountains at our back and get over the top. During the next two nights I would drop down on to the main Rome-Pescara road and walk along it for some twenty miles on each subsequent night. The first day I planned to stay up in the mountains and the next one in a culvert under the main road. I estimated that I should arrive at Pescara on the third morning and buy my ticket on the 8 a.m. to Milan. Our official railway timetable told me exactly when to arrive at the station for the train. This, although a small point, was essential to avoid a long wait before the train came in. From Milan I planned to buy another ticket to Como and from there to get over the Swiss frontier, only about two miles away, at Chiasso. Such was the plan I told to the committee and although they encouraged me, they did not think I had much hope of success. I, for my part, was supremely confident that, given a reasonable degree of luck, I would pull it off and the pessimists made me even more determined that I should succeed.

December 7th was a lovely fine day, and slowly the evening came on. A glorious feeling of tenseness rose up within us like before a race or a parachute jump. My nerves and brain were working at a speed they had nearly forgotten in the previous dulling months. Maps, money and a tiny compass were all concealed in an oilskin package and stuck with sticky plaster well up under my fork. The Italians are delicately minded and could be relied on not to look there.

I pulled on my corduroy trousers and made a bundle of the raincoat and sham Italian uniform. We would put these on at the last moment before going over the wall of the French compound. A battledress jacket covered up my coloured shirt so that in the dark my clothes would pass as reasonable uniform. No badges of rank were worn because we were going to be in both the private soldiers' and the N.C.O.s' compound and might well be seen by one of the more alert carabinieri patrols. Christopher was dressed likewise, and on the evening of the 7th as soon as darkness had fallen, we ate a good meal and went down to the N.C.O.s' compound arriving there about 9 p.m. We had two hours before the moon rose and we planned to start out about 10 p.m. Hurriedly and nervously we dressed in a hut, watched over by the faithful Clements and Lawley. In the meantime an excellent C.S.M. (Company Sergeant-Major) was watching the wall into the French compound and to our chagrin the carabinieri patrol stood under the wall talking to each other from ten minutes to ten until nearly half-past. Already light was beginning to come from the rising moon still below the horizon, and we decided we would have to go back to our compound and try again the next night. We left our escape clothes in bundles in the N.C.O.s' compound, and at about 10:50 p.m. we started back. Christopher got over the wall all right and I was just about to follow, and was actually hanging by my hands from the top, when I heard shouting behind and carabinieri came running up. I would not be able to pull myself up and drop over the other side in time, so I dropped back into the N.C.O.s' compound and decided to make a run for it. I had not taken a dozen paces before I tripped up and went flat on my face. The two Crows pounced on me from behind. In a true Italian way I was led off with the muzzle of a rifle drilling the small of my back with its owner screaming at me in high-pitched Italian, saying I would get twenty-eight days on bread and water. I thought I would, too. As I was wearing no badges of rank I was mistaken for an other rank and I for my part was in no hurry to advise them differently until after I had been searched.

We arrived at the guard room and I was then searched fairly well, all seams being felt through, but my package remained concealed and eventually I was led off and dumped in an other ranks' cell. My name soon trickled through to the Italian officers and I was yanked out and taken back to the officers' compound because all the officers' cells were full. I was in real luck this time because I would be able to have another try next night unless they made room for me the following day in the cells.

Fish-Eyes, the interpreter, had great pleasure in calling me out at the roll-call the next morning and telling me that I would have twenty-one days' solitary confinement as soon as there was room. "Just to make sure you have a happy Christmas," he said as an afterthought. I was furious with the horrible little man, but outwardly I hope I showed a blank face and went away to discuss with Christopher the plans for the night's work. We decided to go through with the same timings because it would give us an extra hour as the moon rises one hour later each night.

All went well. We arrived down at the N.C.O.s' compound after a big send-off from Tag and Gerry Daly.

By this time many knew that we were up to something, but very few knew what we proposed to do. I remember Gerry Daly and Nigel Strutt gave us a wonderful meal of Canadian Red Cross biscuits and cheese and butter, followed by some soused herrings. Not exactly a Lord Mayor's banquet, but it was a feast for us and we were to need every ounce of energy in the days to come. Because of our method of getting out, which involved sidling along an eight-inch wide ledge with a wire fence on one side, we both decided that we could not afford to bulge ourselves out with supplies of food. I took only two packets of biscuits and a pound of chocolate. Later on I discovered that thirst and not hunger was to be my principal enemy. On my timetable it would be five days before I crossed into Switzerland and anybody can go without food for five days and feel none the worse for it.

Soon we had dressed with our mock Italian overcoats and hats covering our semi-civilian get-up. An N.C.O. stood by with the ladder waiting for the moment when the carabinieri were at the farthermost point from where we were to cross into the French compound. We were both a bit nervous at this stage, but I at any rate had complete confidence in the successful outcome of our scheme. It was like walking round the paddock before riding in a point-to-point. My heart was beating a bit faster and nerves were taut whilst waiting for the signal to move off to the start. Only here our stakes were sky high. We both knew that if we failed we would be in solitary confinement for at least twenty-eight days, and it would be a minimum of six months before we would be able to think up another way out.

A hushed whisper of "It's O.K." started us moving. We used the ladder to help us over the wall and dropped down into the French compound. We quickly walked across accompanied by Pierre, and put our ladder against the bottom wall, the other side of which was the passage in front of the Italian guard room and canteen. A quick glance over the top to make sure there was no sentry, and we both dropped silently over. However, in so doing, we had not allowed for the broken glass on top of the walls, and we both cut our hands quite badly. We lay down in the shadow and bandaged them before taking on the next hurdle.

We then stood up and, carrying our ladder with coils of flex and electric light bulbs held prominently in front of us, we went straight for the open door which led into the corridor which separated the guard room from the canteen. The doors leading into the canteen and guard room were both ajar, but without looking into either we walked straight through, and past the sentry outside who made no effort to challenge us. So far so good, and it gave us encouragement for what we knew were going to be the far harder tasks ahead. Everything was so normal that it was almost uncanny. Sentries were in their boxes, perimeter lights outlined the edge of the camp and a faint noise of some concert came from one of the compounds. The sky was starlit, and this it was which gave us the most worry. We had counted on a clouded night in our planning, but we had taken the decision for better or for worse and now we were on our way. There was certainly no going back and we walked grimly on, each of us wondering what the next few seconds would have in store. We came level with the end of the half-completed football field and turned down towards the fateful lamp. I could see the sentry quite clearly outlined against his box and a moment later we were standing underneath the light. Christopher put the ladder against the wall and I climbed up. As I was climbing up the sentry shouted something to us and my heart missed a beat. However we had thought of this and I shouted back, "*Lampa*," in as confident a voice as I could muster for the occasion. We counted on the dumbness of the average Italian soldier not to start questioning us but to accept the extraordinary fact that in the middle of the night we were about to change a bulb that was already burning perfectly. I was always confident on this point in our plans, but many to whom I have told this story can hardly believe it to be true. The reactions of the enemy sentry is as important a subject to study as any other.

By this time I was at the top of the ladder and soon unscrewed the bulb. I made pretence of changing them and screwed the same one back, but only half-way. Now came the crucial test. We had to move sideways along ten yards of ledge, between the bottom of the wall where our ladder was and the outside wire, without arousing the sentry's suspicions. We then made our only mistake. We had decided that, on a really dark night, we could carry the ladder out along this ledge and drop it down outside without the sentry seeing anything. We were so obsessed with this plan that we did not make any allowance for the starlit sky and we tried to go through with our original scheme. I climbed half-way down the ladder and side-stepped on to the ledge and moved about a yard along it at the same time signalling to Christopher to come up the ladder on to the ledge too. Then came the tricky business that we had rehearsed mentally, of Christopher reached down with one hand, catching hold of the ladder at the point of balance and passing it to me to hold. We started to move slowly along the ledge. Our coats seemed to catch in the barbed wire and seconds, which seemed like hours, elapsed before we could free each other. We had just arrived level with the first row of barbed wire when the sentry came running up from his box and started screaming at us. Christopher realised the game was up a fraction of a second before I did and shouted at me to throw the damn' thing away. If it hadn't been for the ladder we could both have dropped down outside by the time this happened. I tossed the ladder away and it landed across three rows of wire which were now beneath us. It came down with a crash and the wires set up a twanging noise that must have been heard all over the camp. The sentry must then have realised that it was up to him to stop us, and he fired a shot. Something flicked past my cheek, and I could feel the sting and blood started to run. By this time I was hanging by my hands to the parapet on the outside of the camp and had dropped into the road outside. The sentry had only managed to get off one round and as this had apparently grazed me, I assumed Christopher was all right and walked straight off. Our plans were to divide immediately on dropping outside the camp and so confuse any pursuers.

I heard later that Christopher had been hit in the thigh by the same shot that had grazed my cheek. The Italians, unknown to us, had issued their sentries with a type of bullet that disintegrated on its way down the barrel and came out in fragments about the size of buckshot. One of the fragments had grazed me, but most had gone into Christopher's leg. He did not even utter a murmur or make any sign to me when we both dropped down outside. He knew that I should have stayed with him for at least a few seconds if I had known and he waited till I was out of sight before calling for help. An artery was punctured and he was ill from loss of blood for a week or two, but luckily he was fully recovered a month later.

As I walked rapidly away it gradually dawned on me that I had actually succeeded in getting out and I was now on the high road to freedom. I now had to prove that I could get to Switzerland. A determination seized me to make it or bust in the attempt. What a thrill it was, and I chuckled to myself when I thought of old Fish-Eyes' face when he realised that the man to whom he had just given twenty-one days' solitary confinement, had got out of his camp on the following night.

My plan was to circle the camp round to the left so that any who saw me whilst I was still nearby would not know in which direction I had gone. Soon I was striking up the mountain at the back with fearful looks over my shoulder in case any guards were already on my trail. My imagination kept telling me that those flashes of light on the hillside below were coming up after me and this spurred me on to ever greater speed. With my breath all gone I eventually decided that I was safe and sat down on the mountainside. The camp stood out like a rectangular Blackpool with all its searchlights blazing and I could imagine checks going on all night to see who had got away, with everybody doing their best to annoy and hinder, and the Italians getting more and more infuriated.

On and up the mountain I went, steering due north by the pole star, and the outline of the valley below. The moon was just rising and soon the whole hillside was lit as clear as daylight. The snow on the hills just above me stood out in startling whiteness and I could see the snowy peaks of the Gran Sasso range thirty miles away to the north. The hillside up which I was labouring was covered with small thorn bushes and some of these caught in my mackintosh and coat, causing triangular rents that would not help my appearance later on. I sat down for another rest just short of the snowline and ate some chocolate, washing it down with a lump of snow, a most unsatisfying sort of drink but certainly better than nothing. My seat felt very cold and I suddenly realised that my beautiful home-made corduroy trousers had split all the way up the back seam. I had no cotton to mend it and so it looked as though I would have to go through Italy with an enormous hole in my trousers and this would not help when it came to bluffing on to the train. I tried without much success to wash the blood off my face with melted snow, so that at least I should look reasonably presentable if I had to walk through a village.

At first I tried walking up through the snow, but mental and physical reactions were beginning to tell and I decided to skirt the mountain just beneath the snow line and to drop down on to the Sulmona-Pescara road just beyond Popoli, which was a tiny village at the head of the gorge leading out of the Sulmona valley towards Pescara. At last I climbed over a spur of the main ridge and could see round the corner down the Pescara valley. The country changed a little here and became steeper and more rugged with great jagged outcrops of rock, which did not help a poor footsore traveller like myself. Pinewoods grew on any available soil and would have been lovely to walk through with their heavenly smell and a glorious view through the trees in any more normal situation. For me every yard was another towards freedom. But with every yard I felt more and more tired! My right foot was aching horribly and I remembered that it had hurt me a little when I dropped over the final parapet out of the camp. I must have landed on a sharp stone and bruised the underside of my foot.

Eventually, at about five o'clock in the morning, I decided it was time to find a place in which to lie up during the following day. The pinewoods were attractive, but newly-cut trees suggested that woodcutters were at work, and I might be discovered by them in daylight. The undergrowth in the pinewoods was anyhow very sparse and it would have been difficult to find a good hiding place. I decided that the best spot would be in one of the scattered clumps of juniper bushes that grew here and there over the whole hillside. Nobody would be likely to stumble on my hiding place as there were so many bushes from which to choose. It would also seem an unlikely place to hide if they tried to follow me up the mountain. Eventually I found a good-sized bush and crept in underneath. After a little scraping with my hands I had my legs covered with dead foliage and with my green Italian overcoat over my head, I must have been nearly invisible. I then settled down to a little sleep and did not wake up until about 11 a.m. when I felt rather cold and cramped. The rhythmic tap of the woodcutter's axe and an occasional splintering sound as another pine tree crashed to the ground, were the only noises to disturb the peace. I stretched my legs and tried to make myself more comfortable, at the same time looking out from my perch on the hillside to get a wonderful view over the sunny valley. The snow was only a few hundred feet above me and out of the sun it was bitterly cold. I attempted to eat some chocolate and biscuits but my mouth was so dry that I could not get them down and I wished that I had a waterbottle with me even at the expense of some of the chocolate.

It was about midday when I heard the tinkling bells of a flock of goats getting nearer and nearer as they fed. I could only hope there was no dog with the goat-herd. I felt safe from anything except a dog. The goats were now grazing all round my bush and here came an old man. A typical Italian of the peasant class, with an old lined weather-beaten face, black coat, sackcloth cape and dirty black trousers, which had been patched everywhere. He came straight for my bush and seemed to look straight at me. My heart stood still for a moment, while I rapidly thought out what I would do if I were discovered. I decided to reason with him to the best of my ability, and as soon as he had gone away I would get as far away from the spot as possible. At that time in Italy, nobody, not even the shepherds and peasants, would lift a little finger to help an escaped prisoner of war. This had been proved by Dan O'Regan when he went for a ten day walk in the hills near Sulmona before being given away by an old woman. Everybody lived in terror of the Questura, which was a type of Italian Gestapo, and it was just not worth their while to help an enemy prisoner of war. The Italians at that time could see absolutely no virtue in helping an obviously defeated enemy, as they thought us then, especially as such an action might easily cost them their life, or at best a long term of imprisonment. This attitude was to change radically after the armistice, when it was brought home to all Italians that they had in fact lost the war, and the fear of the Questura was removed. They could then see that by helping an escaper they might gain favour with the new order, which would pay a good dividend later on.

The old man sat down with his back to my bush and only a yard or so away. There was no dog, which was a mercy and my very breath sounded like steam escaping from a boiler which he could not fail to hear. I did not dare to move my legs which were getting more and more cramped, or shift my position at all. He stayed there about two hours, but then got up and wandered away with his goats down the hillside. I breathed a heartfelt sigh of relief and decided that my luck was in after all and that it was a good omen for the rest of the journey.

Chapter VIII

BY ROAD AND RAIL

LITTLE BY LITTLE the tapping in the woods petered out and eventually all was silent as dusk fell. There were no houses at that height and all the peasants who worked up there probably lived in one or other of the villages down in the valley. When it was quite dark, I got up and stretched myself and massaged my stiff muscles back to life. I was looking forward to some exercise to warm my cold hands and feet and also to a drink from a stream. I started off and stumbled my way along a track that I had seen being used by the old goat-herd when he went down the hill. I was now as high as I need be and would be able to drop down on to the main road running through the gorge. First of all I tried going across the grain of the hillside, but it became more and more broken and I was using up so much energy clambering over the rocks that, when I hit a well-worn track leading straight down the mountain, I decided to take it. The general direction seemed about right although it might bring me nearer to Popoli than I intended. As it turned out it led straight to Popoli, through a series of crevices and ravines with vertical rock faces on either side that gave me no choice but to follow the track and hope for the best. After three hours' walking I crossed a brow and there was Popoli, not a couple of hundred feet below me. It was obvious that I would have to go right through the village to get to the main road on the other side. The time was 9 p.m. and so there should be plenty of people in the streets, through which I hoped to pass unnoticed. My only worry was if they put a check on the outskirts of the village to stop all travellers. I decided to risk this as it was a main road and therefore should have many like myself walking along it. In Italy there are a lot more law-abiding citizens that rely on Shanks' Pony than in England, and it is not uncommon to see men and women walking from village to village by night. The dangerous time was, of course, between about 11 p.m. and 4:30 a.m., and I decided that I would not walk between those hours when I might well be the only one on the road. However I still had two hours of exercise ahead of me before 11 p.m., and that would be plenty.

My track led straight into the village and soon I had the high walls of houses on either side and the road dropping by steps every six feet or so. It was very smelly and there were no doors leading on to it from the houses, but I was determined not to appear a stranger and walked on unconcernedly. I was sharply brought to my senses when a window banged open high up in a house overhanging my road and a bucket full of human excrement just missed me. It suddenly dawned on me that I was walking through the town's main sewer, and, all my pride lost, I retraced my steps and found another way through to the centre of the town without attracting any attention. The humour of the situation was a little lost as I cursed myself for being an unobservant bloody fool.

Coming out of a side street, I turned on to a main road which was full of people, and, guessing the way, continued to walk with as much confidence as I could muster through the town. I did not appear to excite any abnormal interest and I was soon clear of the houses and walking along the main road which ran through a steep-sided ravine alongside the Pescara River. My walk that night was uneventful and on several occasions I passed two or three Italian soldiers on the road without exciting any attention. Many a long drink I had from watering troughs which are on the side of every main road, and I felt I could not absorb enough water to satisfy my needs. I wanted to get to within twenty-five kilometres of Pescara that evening, which would leave quite a short walk for the following night, and I just did it by 11:45 p.m. Almost on the twenty-five kilometre stone there was a large dry culvert running under the main road, which was about six inches deep in dead leaves. It was the ideal hiding place and right on my route for the next night's walk. Footsore and weary I dragged myself inside, and covering myself as best I could with leaves went into the deep sleep of the mentally and physically exhausted.

Numbness and cold woke me just as it was getting light at about 6:30 a.m., and I tried to do some P.T. and massage my stiff muscles back into life again. My only worry was school children. They might start playing around my hiding place and discover me, but again my luck was in and I was bothered by nobody. By nightfall, after a very cold and boring day, I was still safe and undiscovered in my culvert. My plan was to walk to within five or six kilometres of Pescara and then rest near there till about 6 a.m. the following morning. I would then have two hours to walk in and catch the 8 a.m. to Milan with the minimum time to wait about on the platform.

My foot was hurting quite a lot now and, with a steady limp, I trudged along the main road resting every half hour or so and taking a drink when I could. That twenty kilometres seemed never ending, but now I was in the coastal plain and there were many more houses flanking the road. The nearer I came to Pescara the more populated it became and I was getting quite worried about finding a resting place near enough to the town. Fortunately the country opened up a little and soon after the six kilometres stone I found a ploughed field at least four hundred yards from any house and lay flat on my back in a furrow in the centre of the field. It would be a very unlikely place to be stumbled on by accident in the middle of the night and it would do till the following morning as I would be on my way by daybreak. I remember the cold very vividly, but otherwise the night was uneventful.

By 4 a.m. I was getting myself ready. A dry scrape with a razor to remove the worst of my beard—nobody is very fussy in Italy—and my Italian overcoat was pushed into a ditch after it had been used to rub most of the mud off my boots and trousers. The mackintosh was a little bedraggled with its small triangular rents caused by the thorn bushes in the mountains, and streaks of blood from my cheek. By rubbing the material between the palms of my hands I managed to remove most of the bloodstains and my corduroy trousers were similarly treated. The sticking plaster holding my maps and money was unstuck from between my legs and some money carefully folded into the breast pocket of my coat where I would not have to fumble for it when buying my ticket. My Swastika badge was clipped into my buttonhole, and I had my faked German passport in my pocket. This latter document was a product of the imagination of Sandy Clayton, and I don't suppose bore any relation to the real thing. However it looked good and had plenty of rubber stamps and German and Italian signatures authorising nearly everything.

By 5:45 a.m. I was as ready as I could be and started slowly along my last lap to Pescara, which I reached at 7 a.m. I stopped the first woman I saw and asked her the way to the station in halting Italian, introducing my question by *io sono Tedesco* (I am a German). The station was right at the north end of the town and on the other side of the Pescara River. To walk right through an enemy town in daylight was quite amusing, and gave me confidence in my dress. Nobody took the slightest notice and there were plenty of other people carrying a little black bag on their way to work somewhere. Whenever I went anywhere in Italy I always contrived to carry something in my hands. It gave me a *raison d'être* and anybody looking at me obviously thought that my bag was my excuse for going somewhere. Nobody walks anywhere or travels long distances without at least a small bag. Mine was actually a British army officer's satchel made of canvas webbing, dyed in blue-black ink, and looked good enough.

At twenty minutes to eight by the station clock I walked into the main entrance of Pescara station past two carabinieri on duty by the door, and joined a queue at the ticket office. Nobody seemed to take much notice of me, but I saw two more carabinieri standing behind the ticket-inspector at the gate leading on to the platforms. A five hundred lire note was in the palm of my hand and I was now only two places away from the ticket office window. Silently I mouthed my oft-repeated phrase for getting a ticket and my pulse seemed to hammer away in my forehead at a terrific rate. I felt everybody's eyes upon me as I took my turn and uttered a barely audible *"terzo Milano,"* at the same time pushing my five hundred lire note over the counter. Before I knew where I was, a ticket and change were pushed at me and the man behind me was asking for his destination. The blood rushed back into my cheeks, and with renewed confidence I quickly followed the man in front on to the platform, brandishing my ticket in front of me as my passport. The ticket-inspector punched my ticket and said *terzo*-something or other in my ear, which I took to mean Platform 3, and after walking over the railway lines I joined a few others also waiting for the same train. A book-stall was selling papers and I bought a copy of *Signal* which was a German propaganda illustrated paper and published in each language all over Europe. This would act as a further outward and visible passport in addition to my fair hair and Swastika badge. I felt I was now the complete Hun and kept a little aloof from the rest of the passengers to heighten the illusion. The time was now 7:55 a.m. and the train was due in five minutes. My timing could not have been better and so far everything had gone completely according to plan.

The train came in five minutes late and I had soon found a corner seat which I was fated to sit in for the next fourteen hours, all the way to Milan. To my horror a couple of carabinieri came into the same compartment and sat down one next to me and one opposite. Questions went racing through my head. "Had I been spotted and were these two following me?" "Were they going to arrest me then and there?" My confidence came back when one of them cleared his throat in the true Italian style and spat on the floor, rubbing the spittle in with the toe of his boot. He was obviously settling down and apparently I was not under suspicion yet. Three other civilians were in the same compartment and they all added to the quota of spitting that was to continue all the way to Milan at a regular spit per man per ten minutes. I arrived at this average after close study and timing for the first three hours, and I was delighted to see that the average held all the way, in spite of changes in the occupants at various stations. One horribly over-talkative creature tried to speak to me and find out who I was to satisfy his curiosity. In halting Italian I told him I was working on German destroyers at Taranto and was on leave to Germany to see my family. Everybody in the compartment seemed to take quite an unnatural interest in my doings and I cursed them under my breath for their curiosity. However it was all very well meant and certainly nobody seemed to have any suspicions that I was not who I said I was. Nearly every siding had German coal trucks in them and every time the talkative one saw this he pointed it out and said, *Tedesco—buono.*" Eventually he got out and the other occupants left me in peace. Every time a new occupant got in, one of the older ones would nudge him and whisper *Tedesco* in his ear at the same time as nodding at me. I was worried if we should meet a German-speaking Italian, but I was fairly confident as educated Italians practically never travel third class, and Germans in uniform would never do so.

One of the occupants in my carriage leant out of the

window at one of the stations and bought a "*cistina*." This is a cardboard box containing a roll, a leg of chicken, an orange and a bit of cheese. The smell nearly drove me mad with a reawakened hunger, and I decided to risk buying one at our next station, which was to be Bologna. Sure enough a trolley was pushed along the train and I bought a cistina for nine lire. I have hardly ever enjoyed a meal so much and I could barely restrain myself from eating even the orange peel. This was to be my one and only meal on the whole journey, and I could have eaten half a dozen with ease except for the suspicion it might have caused.

My confidence was increasing with every mile and when at last, at about 9:45 p.m., we started to go through Milan suburbs, my morale could not have been higher. I could only hope for a train on to Como without much delay. A sudden doubt crossed my mind that they might have a more thorough check at a big terminus like Milan, but I tried to reassure myself that where there was a crowd I should be safe. Eventually the train pulled in to a platform in Milan Central Station at 10 p.m. and everybody got out on to the platform. The ticket-collector by the barrier had two or three carabinieri standing by him, but there was such a crowd that they would not have much chance and were probably only looking for people without tickets trying to give them the slip.

In some ways Milan Central is rather like a small Waterloo, and the same system was employed to indicate arrivals and departures of trains. I discovered that the last train for Como had left ten minutes previously and I was in a complete quandary what to do till 7 a.m. the following morning when the next one was due to leave. An awful reaction set in as a result of the anti-climax to my plans and in a fit of over-confidence I decided to spend the night in an hotel in Milan. I told myself that if I could get away with it on a train journey, I could surely do the same in an hotel. I suppose this idiotic decision was partly due to my tired mental and physical state, and partly to an over-powering over-confidence that seems to grip escapers as they get close to freedom. Switzerland is only twenty miles from Milan. However, be that as it may, I walked down the long flight of steps from the platform level to the main booking-hall and went straight up to a porter and asked him for the name of an hotel where I could stay the night, introducing my halting Italian by telling him I was German. He immediately gave me a name and a little urchin was button-holed and told to lead me there. I remember how we stumbled across the blacked-out square outside the station and then went down a small street to the right to find the entrance about two hundred yards farther on. The name of the hotel was "Vittoria."

The receptionist was standing behind his desk, and once more my halting Italian came out, asking for a room and some coffee to be sent up. To my horror he answered me in German! He was obviously an Austrian or Tyrolean and that was why I had been sent to this hotel. I mumbled back something in the schoolboy German I had learnt while in prison, and his only answer was, "You are no German"—in German. My pulse beat a bit faster but I determined to have my say and told him, *"Ich bin ein Sudetener—Heil Hitler."* This seemed to satisfy him and he pushed across a card for me to fill in, which I did giving the details of my bogus identity card, which to my horror he asked to look at. He shook his head and said he had never seen one like that before, but I hurriedly interjected that it was for Sudeteners, of course. He then led me upstairs to a comfortable room with a bath next door. Five minutes later a cup of coffee came up on a tray and as the door closed I wolfed it down. I decided to have a rough wash down before going to bed and never have I enjoyed a cold bath more. There was no spare fuel for unnecessary luxuries like hot baths in Italy at this time. After I had dried myself and had another scrape with the razor, I began to look almost respectable. Then I collapsed on the bed in a state of semi-exhaustion.

In spite of being tired in every limb, I began to reflect on what the receptionist had said. My brain at last started to work, and I suddenly realised what an absolute idiot I had been. The man had obviously realised I was not who I said I was, and was probably even now telephoning to police Headquarters for someone to come round and look me over. I decided to dress and leave the hotel straightaway and my clothes flew on to my body as quick as lightning. I went downstairs; it was only a small pension hotel; and the same man was sitting at his desk, and not unnaturally, seemed a little surprised to see me. I mumbled something about making a mistake in my train timings and put down thirty lire for my bed. He got slowly up from his seat and said quite softly in German, "You are not a Sudetener, you are an Englishman." I drew myself up as best I could and asked for my change, and told him he was not only making a fool of himself but was being very impertinent. This seemed to take him aback, but he still looked very suspicious and asked me where I was going. I told him "Torino" which was the direction diametrically opposite to Como and also quite likely to have a train in the middle of the night. He slowly pushed the change across, and trying hard not to hurry, I put it in my pocket and walked out of the door. It was a narrow squeak, and I am sure he had asked for the police to come and investigate. I could feel it in the tone of his voice. With shaking knees I walked straight back to the station and decided to spend the rest of the night in the waiting-room. This was big and half-full already with sleeping bodies. It was the ideal place to hide away until morning.

At 6 a.m. I went down to the main booking-hall for my ticket to Como and was cheered up when out it came as easily as before. Back upstairs and into the third class buffet for three cups running of steaming hot *caffè al latte*. It was synthetic coffee, but it was hot and wet, and tasted wonderful. After the coffee the inevitable happened, and I was seized with a desire to relieve myself and walked round to the public lavatory in the station. As in all continental lavatories an old woman was in charge, and she took fifty centisimi before going ahead and indicating an open door. I must have looked pretty scruffy because she thought I was an illiterate peasant and started a loud harangue on the merits of the lavatory which embarrassed me not a little. The peasant Italian much prefers the squat type without any seats, but this one had both available. The squatters were all occupied and perforce the old woman had to show me one of the seat type. Seeing that I looked a little blank at her harangue, she demonstrated how to sit on the seat, and loudly told me that a seat was for sitting on and not standing on. Milan had a very modern station, the pride of Fascist architecture. It even had lavatories *"di nuovo tipo,"* as the old woman put it!

I stepped aboard the 7 a.m. electric train for Como and was soon rattling out of Milan towards the frontier. My only worry was that there might be a check on all trains going towards Switzerland, but I was in luck. My spirits were rising with every minute and in a few minutes we were passing through countryside that was looking hillier and more alpine in texture every minute. We stopped at every station and anxiously I looked out to see any signs of police boarding the train to check papers, but there was none in sight. At last we pulled into Como station and the lake was just visible over the houses to the north. The ticket-collector took the ticket and I walked straight past the scrutinising glare of some more carabinieri. I was now on the last lap, but unfortunately I had the whole day to spend before starting towards the frontier at nightfall.

This was my second mistake. I should have remained in Milan all that day and come on to Como at dusk. As it was, I had been so keen to get out of Milan after the hotel incident that I took the first train in the morning. Como and its area was suburban and it was going to be very difficult to find a hiding place for the day. I was soon walking through the streets towards the north and realised I should have to go some way before finding a path off the main road into the country. A little farther along I could see my road climbing a small hill, half-way up which there appeared to be a possible turning-off. When about three hundred yards from the road junction, I saw two frontier guards coming in the opposite direction dressed in their alpine uniform. I don't know why it was, but I had a feeling

that all was not going to be well before I came up to them,
but on the other hand I thought it would look even more
suspicious if I turned round and retraced my steps. I
thought I might just make the turn off before reaching the
two soldiers, in which case they would hardly have a
chance to stop me. How I afterwards cursed that decision!
I could easily have turned about when they were still two
or three hundred yards away and they would never have
been any the wiser.

To cut a long story short, they stopped me and asked
me where I was going. Having blustered a bit, I showed
them my papers, but very politely I was told that I would
have to come along to their H.Q. which was only a few
hundred yards away. This I did, and was given a drink
of wine while I waited. Eventually I was told that I would
have to be taken to the frontier post because there was
somebody there who could talk German. My heart felt
suddenly very heavy. I might perhaps give them the slip
on the way, but my foot hurt quite a lot now and I would
not have had a chance against two fit Alpinis. If only it had
been dark it might have been easy to make a dash for freedom, but it was broad daylight and about twelve o'clock
on a glorious sunny and cloudless day.

We boarded a trolley-bus which took us down to the
frontier post at Chiasso, a village half in Switzerland and
half in Italy. The main road had a huge barricade on the
frontier, with the frontier post just beside it. I half-knew
the game was up, but determined to put up a show till the
last. As I was ushered into a room where a dirty little weed
of an official, wearing an outsize chauffeur's cap and horn-
rimmed spectacles, was sitting behind a desk, I gave him

a heel-click and *"Heil Hitler."* It was still just faintly possible that his German would have been worse than mine, but hardly likely. It wasn't!

Almost at once he had sized me up and told me I was English and asked me who I was—in English. I told him my name and, on looking down a list, he discovered mine amongst some others. Quite surprising efficiency for Italians, and all the frontier posts must have had the warning. I was then searched and nothing was discovered except some money, as I had chucked my maps away when walking with the two Alpinis.

The little comic-opera official seemed highly delighted at his capture, and became quite affable. "There will be promotion all round for this," he said, and asked me if I would like anything to eat. I told him I could eat a horse. I also asked him if the two soldiers who stopped me knew why they had done so. The two men seemed rather at a loss to know why, but one said that it was my general appearance, above all my dirty boots! Another lesson learnt and not to be forgotten in future attempts.

I was put into another room, with two guards watching me, and a meal was soon brought in from a local restaurant. I remember its savour to this day, but my enjoyment was tempered by the thought that I had got so near and yet so far. Even then I was within twenty yards of Swiss soil and this might be my last chance in the war to be so close, and it would certainly be six months before I should be able to have another try.

I have never been so depressed, before or since. My world, which had been getting brighter and brighter, was now inky black. Although I can usually make the best of most things, I found my present plight difficult to stomach. While I sat moping, I dropped off to sleep in fits and starts and hoping the guards would follow suit; but it had no effect and they remained as watchful as ever.

After about two hours, three plain-clothes policemen came in and I was hustled into a waiting car and driven off very fast down the main road to Milan. I had a good look at the frontier wire before going and also the scenery. My luck might hold and I might be back in the area trying to cross the frontier again one day.

Driving through Milan was interesting and I could see no signs of bomb damage. The town looked like a rather dirty version of one of our own midland towns, but with the usual continental touch of cafés on the pavements and paper kiosks at street corners.

The car stopped outside an impressive building which proved to be Police H.Q., and I was hustled into a small room with two fat carabinieri looking on. They had a paper and started to bait me with its news. Japan, they said, was now fighting us, and already she had sunk the whole American Navy at Pearl Harbour and two British battle-ships. England was in a hopeless position, they chorused and ended by a *"Viva Duce. Duce e forte."* All this was news to me, but I pretended I knew all about it and told them it was all propaganda and lies. *"Tutte mensogne,"* I told them. "Look," I said, "how your papers lied about the Eritrean and Libyan fighting, and see where we are now. The British always win the last battle, as your own Garibaldi used to say."

This seemed to surprise them as I had not obviously taken their propaganda as had been intended, and instead of being depressed had actually had the impertinence to say the British would win in the end. However, with an angry *"Duce e forte, Duce e forte,"* they stopped trying to tease me and sat glumly looking down the barrels of their rifles. Just occasionally the fatter of the two would draw himself up and shout his *"Duce e forte"* chorus again and then sit down, as though constantly to reassure himself that his Duce really was strong and all-powerful. At last I was shown into a cell and told I would be questioned in the morning. There was a pile of straw in one corner, which I soon spread out and, with two blankets round me, slept the sleep of the truly weary both in body and spirit. What a day it had been, so full of hope and confidence, only to be dashed to the ground and broken into a thousand pieces. My life seemed to have crumbled about me but my weary bones at last overcame my spirit. All this happened on December 13th, 1941.

Chapter IX

SOLITARY CONFINEMENT

M‌Y INTERROGATION started next morning and went on more or less continuously for over twenty-four hours. I was put on a hard seat with a powerful flood-lamp shining in my face. A little, suave man was sitting behind a desk and first he started pleading and coaxing. "All I want to know," he said, "is the name of the Italian who helped you to get to the frontier." They just could not believe that anybody could have reached the frontier without help; but in order to mystify him and prevent any tightening up in the railway regulations, I told him, "I can't say." This answer became mechanical and I must have repeated myself thousands of times during the questioning. After four hours his relief came in and started off with the brilliant idea that I could be bribed into telling. "If only you will give me the name of the Italian," he said, "you can choose the camp you go to, be it by the sea or up in the mountains, or in the south."

So it went on all the morning until midday when I said: "I am sick of all this nonsense. I want some lunch."

"You can have some lunch when you answer my questions like a gentleman should."

"You know perfectly well that I will not answer your

damn silly questions. If you won't give me anything to eat, which I may remind you is contrary to the Geneva Convention, then please allow me to use the lavatory."

"All right and I will look forward to seeing you this afternoon after I have had my own lunch."

After relieving myself, I was put back in the cell for an hour or so, and then the whole performance started over again, and went on continuously till the evening when one of them lost his temper.

"You filthy Englishman sitting there so smiling. Roma has telephoned to say that any methods can now be used. If necessary you will be shot as a spy, and for wearing the uniform of our army."

"That won't help me answer your questions."

"Oh, you think yourself funny, do you. So. You will now stand up and answer, do you hear me, *answer* my questions."

He ended in a high-pitched scream and told the soldier behind me to take away my chair and keep the muzzle of his rifle in my back.

All night long the same old questions were put to me. Sometimes he used a quiet voice, appealing to my better judgment and what he called my "instincts as a gentleman." More often he was angry and insulting and shouted at me across his desk. If I tried to move at all, the rifle in my back gave me a hard jab, and by morning had made it very tender. It was several weeks before the soreness wore off.

About dawn the following morning, a burst of firing suddenly came to my ears and it was announced dramatically that yet another British spy had been shot. "Now will you tell us? Surely it is not worth dying to save one of your enemies?"

I told them I was bored, tired and not amused. This of course enraged them and a torrent of invectives came out in rapid Italian before the once-suave interrogator could be calmed down. Then he told the guard to take me away and give me a meal. As I went out of the door, he said with malice that he would see that I would get very special treatment for the next month or two, just to make sure that I did not try and do the same thing again. The grilling had not been enjoyable but it had been an interesting experience of the Fascist police machine at work.

Next morning I went by car to the Central Station between two burly carabinieri and by 9 a.m. was on a train for Piacenza, a small town in the Po valley about seventy miles from Milan. We climbed out at a little station between Alessandria and Piacenza, and had to walk about three miles to my new home by the name of Montalbo. It was here that I was to undergo my solitary confinement for escaping and I actually never went into the main camp itself.

Montalbo was an old castle built on the top of a little hill overlooking the Po plain. An officers' punishment cell had just been built adjoining one wing of the castle, which was surrounded by a narrow perimeter of barbed wire only a few feet away from the walls. At that time Montalbo had only been opened a few months and was for the exclusive use of about eighty officer prisoners of war. Immediately on arrival I was put straight into the cell, accompanied by the usual Italian shouting and screaming whenever things were not quite right.

Life was very uncomfortable, except for the food which was comparatively good and plentiful and came from the officers' kitchen in the main camp. No books were allowed, nor were writing materials or even pencils. I only had half an hour's exercise each day and that in a kind of bird-cage outside the door to my cell. This was about twenty yards long by two yards wide, and was hardly big enough even to stretch my arms let alone swing the proverbial cat. The most exercise that I ever got was to walk to the lavatory in the castle, so that three times a day (the maximum allowed) I had a lovely hundred yards' walk, which was at least a change from my cell.

Whilst eating my lunch on the second day, I discovered under the cabbage a stub of pencil and a note. It told me to write my needs on a piece of lavatory paper the next time I went there and to leave it on top of the cistern. This I did, asking for books. At the same time I said who I was and why I was in a cell. Next time I went to the lavatory I collected a book and hid it under my coat on the way back. The pencil was invaluable and I was soon making up new crossword puzzles complete with clues on pieces of lavatory paper.

A few days after I went into the cell it started to snow, and when it was not snowing, a fog enshrouded our hill, which had the combined effect of making all the walls run with water and also was extremely cold. Everything was damp, and my top blanket was sopping wet with the moisture. As I only had two, I wrapped these around me bundle-wise and, keeping all my clothes on, managed to keep tolerably warm. It was the lack of exercise that did it, of course. If only I had been able to get my circulation going at least once a day, I would have been far better off.

The books lasted till Boxing Day, when the Italians discovered the trick and stopped me using the castle lavatory. All that was offered as a substitute was a quart-sized tomato tin that leaked all over the floor and did not add to the savour of the place. As my boots were given to me only once a day for my half hour's exercise, I was forced to give up my pacing back and forth in the cell because of the muck on the floor. The Italian Commandant occasionally visited me, and when I complained that he was breaking the Geneva Convention by not giving me books, by not allowing me writing material and by failing to take sanitary precautions which rendered my cell unfit to house pigs in, he just laughed and went away.

After I lost the books I took to making up bigger and better crosswords on bits of lavatory paper. I came to the conclusion that making up crosswords was far harder than solving them, and it gave me a mental occupation which stopped me getting too depressed. In between making up crosswords I tried to remember all the poetry I had ever learnt at school and recited it to myself. I found that by concentration I could remember a surprising amount. It gave me an inner satisfaction which helped me to remember that it would not be long before the maximum of thirty days' confinement allowed by the Geneva Convention was up, and I should be free to move around and talk to other men again. My only other brain occupation was multiplying two numbers together in my head. Eventually I found I could multiply two six figure numbers together and then write down the answer and check it on paper. A childish occupation, perhaps, but it helped to pass many a long, weary hour. How I hated the Commandant of that camp! He even refused to let me have a Bible, which I asked for on Christmas Eve. I had previously got hold of one with the other books, but it was taken away when they searched me after discovering the lavatory trick.

Undoubtedly the highlight of my confinement was when, on New Year's Eve, Douglas Schofield and Harry Wakelin were pushed into my cell by a host of carabinieri after much shouting and screaming in the usual manner. Apparently they had both tried to rush out through the knife-rest of barbed wire, which served as a temporary gate, and then had dropped down the twenty-foot wall just outside. Unfortunately they both hurt themselves in their fall. Before they had time to pick themselves up and run away an extremely excited Italian had his rifle levelled at them from six yards' range, his finger trembling on the trigger. They had to give themselves up and were literally thrown into my cell. This was a huge relief to me, but rather cold comfort for them.

Both had most interesting tales to tell and in return I gave them all the information I could about my journey which might help them later on. Douglas Schofield had been caught after a commando raid in which he had blown up a bridge in northern Sicily, but he had failed to find the submarine *Triumph* afterwards in his canoe. He had been out on five patrols in submarines from Malta, and on each occasion he was landed in his collapsible "folbot" to blow up some selected point on the railway line up and down the length of Italy. It was most interesting, he said, to paddle back to the submarine and then wait for the next train to come along and see it blown up on the mine that he had laid, and then watch it tumble down the cliff. He always placed his mines on a bend in the track and the weight of the engine pressing down on the rails set the charge off which made the whole train plunge down the cliff. He was a charming chap, but a bit embittered by prison life, as we all were.

Harry Wakelin had escaped from a temporary prison camp established near Corinth by German parachute troops when Greece was overrun. He then lived a nomad existence in the Greek hills for three months and collected fourteen or twenty British and Cypriot other ranks around him. If he had been by himself he would have had an excellent chance of getting out of Greece by way of Turkey, but the encumbrance of the other ranks was considerable and it was through them that he eventually was caught. His capture was also partly due to a Greek informer who earlier had befriended him and then succumbed to the reward that the Germans had placed on the head of every Britisher brought in alive or dead. His tales of life in the Greek villages and in the mountains were most interesting and sometimes kept us laughing for minutes on end to the annoyance of the guard standing shivering outside.

My thirty days were up on the fourteenth of January, but still the Italians refused to release me. It was not until the nineteenth of January that I was told that I was being taken back to Sulmona, and was to leave straightway. A captain, a lieutenant, and two private soldiers had come up specially to escort the "very dangerous" prisoner back to camp. It was really rather ludicrous, but it gave me satisfaction to realise how troublesome my escape had been to the Italians. They took escapes seriously and made every effort to stop them, which was one of the biggest reasons why we must go on trying and was the only way we had left to help in the war effort.

My guards became quite friendly on the way back, and told me that the Sulmona Commandant had been sent to the Russian front as a result of our escape from the camp. It was surely a very heavy sentence for so mild an offence, they thought. I laughed aloud and they thought it in extremely bad taste. They also told me that Christopher had been wounded, but was now all right. As this was the first news that I had had of it, I could scarcely believe their words, though I was glad to hear that he had recovered.

Evidently my guards thought that I had hopped on to a goods train in the Sulmona valley; they even said that railway guards had seen me doing it! So much the better, I thought to myself, as this would enable me to repeat the same method of getting a ticket the next time I got out.

A car met us at Sulmona station, and I was driven back to the camp from which I had escaped six weeks before. It was almost like coming back home, and great was my welcome by all my friends. In some ways my recapture was a good thing because it provided a whole lot of new information which might be useful to future escapers. It also dispelled the bogey once and for all that it was impossible for anybody to escape and also have a reasonable chance of getting to a neutral country. There could no longer be any excuse for not having a try on that score, and I think it gave confidence to some who had sat on the fence not quite knowing whether to take the plunge or not.

I was so ashamed of my stupidity in the Milan hotel

incident that I never breathed a word about it. It is funny how sensitive one can become in a prison camp, and I somehow felt that I might be branded as an idiot who threw away good chances of success, and therefore should not be allowed to try again.

In two or three weeks I regained my fitness and started to look round for a new way out. As it was now mid-winter and really filthy weather there would be no chance of an escape much before May. During my nosing around I heard of a very exclusive tunnel then under construction, and I wormed my way into the team making it on the excuse that my outside experience would be helpful to all concerned. The tunnel started right up in the north-eastern corner of the top officers' compound, in one of the dormitories. This particular dormitory was only about thirty yards from the wire and so only required a tunnel of about fifty yards which was much shorter than most. The entrance to it was cunningly concealed by four tiles which lifted out of the floor underneath a bed. This lid was made of very solid construction, so that it would not sound hollow if the floor was tapped. During the month I was at Sulmona the room was methodically searched three times, every tile on the floor being tapped and closely examined, and the entrance was not discovered. It led to a deep shaft and from there the tunnel started. It was very hard work, but it kept one amused and I at any rate felt I was doing something to get out.

I had not been back in Sulmona more than a few days when the Italians announced that a special camp for dangerous prisoners was being started near Pisa. Seven officers were to go to it straight away and included both Com-

mander Brown, R.N., and Tag Pritchard. Both these officers were suspected of having organised escapes. They had
not escaped themselves but on this occasion the Italians
were not far short of the truth. I was not included but was
told by the camp officials not to worry as I was certain to
follow as soon as Roma realised that I was back at Sulmona and therefore capable of being moved up to the new
camp. I rather looked forward to going, because not only
was the new camp another three hundred miles nearer
Switzerland than Sulmona, but Sulmona was really getting
a very hard camp from which to get out, except by tunnelling. My marching orders came exactly one month after
getting back to Sulmona and nobody was more pleased
than I.

I heard later that the tunnel, which I had had a small
part in constructing, was successfully completed the following June, and all concerned were just waiting for a
suitable night when a cow outside the wire put her foot on
a thin spot and sank down up to her belly. It was really
bad luck as the project had deserved success. There had
been so many fruitless searches for the entrance, and so
much hope, toil and sweat had been expended on its construction. I also heard that during one search the carabinieri tapped every tile over the whole floor and became
convinced that one tile sounded hollow. The usual great
excitement followed with troops and carabinieri everywhere making spot searches on anybody they thought
looked at all suspicious. A mason was called in and eventually he smashed the offending tile only to discover that the
hollow sound was caused by an air gap under the tile left
by an idle workman when the floor was laid. As soon as

the room occupants, who were all workers in the real tunnel, realised that they were about to dig up the wrong part of the floor, this was exploited with violent expostulations against causing discomfort to defenceless prisoners of war, the Geneva Convention, etc., etc. The carabinieri only redoubled their efforts and were the laughing-stock of the rest of the camp when it was seen that they had been on the wrong scent. This was of course again exploited by the tunnellers, and the carabinieri did not bother them further.

Chapter X

MONASTERY LIFE

A CAPTAIN and a lieutenant acted as escort to take me to Campo 27 between Pisa and Florence, and an Italian private soldier came to carry my kit. By this time I had accumulated quite a lot of luggage. I took with me two suitcases, an army pack, a roll of blankets, and a wooden crate full of books. It never seemed to worry the Italians how much kit we took, since they regarded it as quite normal for officers. Their own took about thirty large trunks, mostly full of different uniforms, wherever they moved, even on active service. A paltry suitcase or two was very small beer by comparison.

We climbed aboard the train for Rome, and apparently orders had been issued that one of the two escorting officers would have a drawn revolver in his hand at all times. It was repeatedly explained to me that if I budged an inch off my seat I should be shot. This was explained in the usual Latin way, with much flourishing of the loaded revolver, and always repeated whenever anybody was within earshot. Having harangued me, my escort would then turn to the audience and tell them that I was a most dangerous prisoner who had escaped over twenty times before, so they must keep well clear. The crowd never believed the story for they were Italians and had themselves told similar

127

stories. They then edged closer to have a good look. The compartment in which I sat was like a booth at a fair, and relays of passengers came in and sat down for a few minutes, while the bravery of the escort in taking such a dangerous criminal on a public train was implied a dozen times to the admiration and disbelief of the onlookers.

Eventually we arrived at Rome at 7 p.m. and my brave Captain announced that we had a three-hour wait before catching the train to Pisa. I told him that the Geneva Convention insisted that all prisoners of war must be reasonably fed, and suggested going to have dinner in an hotel. I had hoped that their attention might be relaxed after a good dinner with plenty of vino and might give me a chance to give them the slip. After a lot of argument, during which I threatened to report him both to the Protecting Power and to the Papal Emissary, the next time they visited our camp, he eventually gave in, and all three of us trooped into the station restaurant. We sat down at a table in the middle and soon the loud voices of my escorts informed all present who I was, while I was ordering the biggest meal I could get out of a fawning English-speaking Italian waiter, who said he had worked in London before the war. I remember we had five courses including whitebait and roast chicken, and two bottles of a good Chianti. My escort, however, was always watchful, and rather shamefacedly he held his revolver under the tablecloth with one hand while attempting to eat with the other. I think they had both been threatened with service in Russia if I should escape, because I have never had a more diligent Italian escort.

At last we got up from the table feeling much better, and

I was led off to a waiting-room until the train came in, an hour late, at 11 p.m. After another three-hour wait at Pisa for a slow train to take us along the line to Florence, we alighted at 6 a.m. at a little station only about half a mile from our new camp and about a third of the distance between Pisa and Florence.

My new home proved to be part of an old monastery. From outside it looked like a prison, and this impression was heightened by the massive iron and oak door leading into the cloisters, whence a bare stone staircase led to the monks' cells, each of which now housed two prisoners of war. In one I found Tag still lying down half asleep and I heard the story of Campo 27 whilst he shaved and dressed.

There were eight British officers including myself, and about thirty Greeks. All the British had come from Sulmona and had either made an escape or had been suspected by the Italians of organising one. The Greek officers were an odd-looking lot. Most had deserted during the war in Albania and were active Italian sympathisers. A few were excellent types, who had been made prisoner after being wounded, and warned us about their brother officers.

"If it wasn't for these Greeks, we would be out of this camp by now, so easy are the obstacles compared with Sulmona. Every scheme we have thought of so far has had to be turned down because the Greeks would give the show away. It is obvious why the Italians have sent us here. The defences are within the camp rather than all round it. But never mind. We have some other ideas, which we hope will bear fruit in a month or two. Let's go and have some breakfast."

We went downstairs to the old monks' refectory hall and

sat down to a breakfast consisting of a large cup of ersatz coffee and two small slices of dry bread. George Patterson came in at the same time and after a ribald greeting said:

"You know, Tony, that bread has to last you all day and weighs exactly 150 grammes to the nearest crumb."

"Don't pull my leg."

"For once I mean it. We are damned hungry, but we don't seem to be much the worse for it yet. The Greeks do all the cooking and as there is only one kitchen and we are in the minority, we have to lump it."

"Do they pinch the rations then?"

"No, I don't think so, but they have no idea how to make the food go a long way, and some of their dishes make us squirm a bit. We haven't had any Red Cross parcels since we arrived here in spite of repeated letters to the Protecting Power and even the Pope."

"It all sounds rather grim."

"Well, it is not too bad really. It is a wonderful change after Sulmona and we are much nearer Switzerland."

George finished his coffee and we went out into the monastery garden to look around. Half the building was still occupied by monks, but brick walls had been built to shut us off completely and all round were the usual sentries, barbed wire and lights. Wherever we went there were Greeks and it was obvious that any scheme to get out would have to include some plan to divert their attention.

Lunch came round and consisted of a plate of vegetable soup and any bread left over from breakfast. Supper was much the same except that the soup usually had about half an inch of rice at the bottom of the plate. On Sundays enough macaroni had accumulated from the daily ration allowance to have a soup plate full each and this was the only comparatively solid meal of the week. Our canteen allowed us half a litre of vino a day and also fruit, if one could afford the high prices charged.

To our great surprise our diet at first seemed to make no appreciable difference to our health, except for an almost continuous hunger pain at the pit of our stomachs. We went out for walks twice a week, and the country was lovely in the spring. Sheltered little farms and vineyards dotted the landscape as if the white houses and red roofs had been shaken out of a giant pepper pot and had landed haphazardly on hill and dale. Young corn gave a bright green sheen to the picture which was only occasionally broken by regular rows of vines or olives. Higher up the hills to the north, were nearly continuous olive groves, with the little town of Lucca, of olive oil fame, only about thirty miles away.

After about six weeks, the effect of the starvation rations began to be noticed. Although we felt quite fit, we no longer had the desire for walks that we had on our arrival, and getting up in the morning began to be more and more of an effort. At Sulmona, Tag had swollen to the most enormous size, in spite of his forty minutes' P.T. every day. At Campo 27 he visibly shrank and in the end was unable to do his P.T., which was an astounding break in his routine. After three months we just wandered listlessly around the garden, praying and hoping for Red Cross parcels. To our delight these turned up unexpectedly soon after. Solid bully beef and biscuits, scrumptious cheese, packets of raisins, chocolate, tea, milk, and even sugar. How we blessed the Red Cross and their parcels! Every mouthful was chewed and chewed and almost regretfully swallowed. We could each of us have polished off a Red Cross box on the spot, but very wisely limited ourselves to one a week, both to spare our digestions, long unused to such fare, and eke out the supply of food. After the arrival of the Red Cross boxes we had smiles on our faces and once more felt hopeful for our future, redoubling our efforts to find a way out which the Greeks would not spot.

One of the Greeks could speak a little English; we called him Peter, and he was an excellent little chap who told us many tales of his country and his home in Athens. One Greek major had fought in the 1914 war against us while acting as interpreter between the Turks and Germans. Apparently he had had a very cosmopolitan education and could speak Turkish and German like his native tongue. Tag and I used to practise our German on him, and in the end we became quite good, thanks to his help.

Pilot Officer "Basher" Beauclair was the first of us to have a try to get out. Short and stocky with a rosy apple complexion, he had a R.A.F. reputation of being slightly mad and willing to have a go at anything. He had been shot down in the Western Desert on almost the first day that Italy declared war, when making a zero level attack in a Blenheim bomber on an Italian airfield.

He had noticed that the main door of the monastery was usually left ajar to allow sentries to pass to and fro. Outside there was only one rather sleepy sentry on duty. Basher thought that he could rush out of the gate and down the road at dusk, and get away in the confusion. I think he would have succeeded, but on passing through the main door he ran slap into the arms of one of the Italian officers who had just come out of his office. It was extremely bad luck, and the officer lost his temper. He stripped off all Basher's clothes, slapped him in the face and sent him back naked to his room—all in front of the Italian private soldiers, who by now had turned out to see the fun. Basher was given the normal thirty days' solitary, and we vowed that if ever a member of the Protecting Power or Red Cross visited our camp we would try to get some official action taken against the Italian.

In spite of repeated demands by us for visits from outside officials, the Italians did not allow them near our camp. They were a little alarmed at the prospects of an investigation, and from the Commandant downwards were scared stiff that any of us should escape because then they might be punished for negligence by being sent abroad to fight.

It was towards the end of our second month that we gradually formulated a plan to get us all out. During those eight weeks Lucky had been piecing together the geography of the other side of the wall, by pretending he was a Roman Catholic and asking to go to confession to one of the monks next door. He was taken round regularly each week, and contrived to be taken back a different way each time. Eventually we had a very clear idea of the layout. The corridors, off which led our bedroom cells, had once upon a time communicated with the rest of the monastery, and we discovered that the wall of an end cell led into a deserted passage on the monks' side. Unfortunately all the cells in this corridor, except for the end one, were occupied by Greek officers and it would have been impossible to tunnel through the wall without the whole passage knowing about it.

The big problem was how to distract the Greeks, while we made the hole. We had a clue to the solution a fortnight later, when the Greeks all celebrated a feast day, and invited us to attend as guests. The party started at about 6 p.m. and went on for thirty-six hours. They had all saved up their vino for a whole month past and drank on and off the whole time. After about twenty-four hours they were decidedly merry and nearly hoarse from singing weird Greek songs and shanties; by 6 a.m. next morning they were all sleeping the sleep of the drunk. What a party! They were quite offended when we tried to go about midnight on the first night. At last we managed to creep out about 2 a.m., when we suddenly realised, to our great surprise, that it was going to go on all through the next day and night. They looked terrible for about a week afterwards.

We decided that we would save up all our wine for the next two months. That should keep them going for at least twelve hours, which would be sufficient for our purpose. Lt. Sullivan, a Naval Swordfish pilot, revealed himself an expert forger and produced the most wonderful identity cards. All the usual paraphernalia of escaping, such as clothes and money, were sorted out, and standard phrases learnt. Our equipment was really first-class, and the plan was to take a train to Florence and from there to Milan and the Swiss frontier. Our chances were excellent once we were clear of the camp.

We drew lots who should make the hole in the wall, and it fell to Commander Brown and me. The chosen day arrived and we started to ply the Greeks with drink as rapidly as possible starting after lunch at about 2 p.m. We reckoned they would be nicely merry by about 9 p.m., when we planned to start work, and we thought we would be through the hole and away by 11 p.m. Although the wall was only of one brick thickness and of fairly soft texture, it was no easy matter to make a hole without any noise. Our instruments were a sharp bit of iron and a carving knife, and we soon realised that the job was not going to be as easy as we thought. As a result we probably made more noise than we had intended.

We had just pushed the point of our instrument through the bricks, when a light was shone on the hole from the other side and somebody was shouting in Italian and banging on the wall. We had obviously been discovered and so ran quickly back to our rooms and gave the alarm. Our kit, maps, food and clothes were quickly hidden, and in a few seconds we had undressed and were lying in bed. Just as we pulled the sheets up the Italians arrived, having taken about five minutes to gather together. We all pretended to turn over sleepily in our beds, but this did not impress the Italians, who were livid. They all talked at once as they went through our rooms with a fine tooth comb. They only found incriminating articles on Tag and George Patterson. The next day poor old Tag and Pat were both doing twenty-eight days' solitary, and I am afraid Commander Brown and I both smiled a little when we realised that it really should have been us behind the bars. If the Italians had been clever and had come round to us silently without flashing torches and banging on the wall, they would have caught both of us red-handed.

Unfortunately we had chosen the one night in the week when a monk cleaned out the chapel. Normally he would have come from the chapel and, crossing a small court-yard, gone back to his cell without coming upstairs near our wall. On this particular night it had been raining and to avoid getting wet he had decided to take the disused corridor. We were all greatly disappointed as we had great confidence in our scheme and with a little more luck it would almost certainly have succeeded.

The local general came down the next day to see what we had been up to, and made a little speech to us in voluble high-pitched Italian in a tiny room that just held the nine of us. He ended up by saying that "He, General Bolo, or-dered us not to escape or even try to escape. We were all officers and we knew what orders were. If we disobeyed these orders, we would be shot." Ending his little speech with a high-pitched shout, he turned about and marched out of the room, followed by the Italian officers from the camp. There was a slight pause and we all had a good laugh. If I had not been there I could hardly have believed that such a Ruritanian comic-opera show could have taken place. It kept us cheered up for quite a long time to come.

Chapter XI

MALINGERING

I⊤ WAS about a month later, at the end of April, that we first heard a rumour that Headquarters in Rome had decided that our camp was not good enough for desperate characters like us, and were opening a really escape-proof prison somewhere in the south of Italy. It turned out later on that this camp was to be the notorious Number 5, which was located even farther north than Campo 27.

Realising that our next camp was going to be no sinecure, I decided that I must make an attempt before the move. But when we were warned on May 7th that we would leave on the 15th, no time remained to plan a new way out of our camp. My only chance seemed to be to get to a hospital whilst still in the north of Italy. I had been operated on for mastoids behind my left ear when I was a boy, and so it was not difficult to pretend extreme pain and deafness. The local doctor said I must see a specialist at once, so the next day I was taken to Florence Military Hospital.

The big snag of the hospital idea was the question of the clothes that I was going to wear when I got out. I would almost certainly be searched on entering the hospital, and any but the simplest of disguises would be impossible to take in with me. As a result of my experiences on the Italian

137

railways six months before, I finally decided that clothes did not really matter as long as they were not obviously uniform. Eventually I took with me to hospital a navy blue roll-neck pullover which my mother had just sent me, battle-dress trousers with the outside pockets removed, and brown shoes. As a hat I had one which had been issued to me by the Italians and was in the form of one of their own field service hats dyed a dark chocolate brown colour; the peak could be pulled down and the straps going over the top of the cap cut off, to make quite a presentable peasant's cap as worn all over northern Italy. My money and maps were in the usual place between my legs and stuck to me with sticking plaster.

The train journey to Florence and the cab ride out to the hospital were uneventful, but I tried to remember the way, especially the direction of the station. The hospital was a large building facing the main Florence-Bologna road, and stood about two miles from the centre of the town. I was hustled up to the top storey and was searched quite thoroughly by a carabiniere who signed for me from my escort. I was then shown into my room, which was not unlike that in many English hospitals and contained three beds.

I was in the hospital for nearly a month and I had quite an amusing time. The food was excellent compared with prison fare, and the Italian nurses were kindness itself. The specialist came on the second day and said he did not think there was much wrong with my ear, but he understood that life in a prison camp might not be very amusing and told me I could stay as long as I liked. Apparently quite a high proportion of the hospital patients had little the matter with them, but the doctors encouraged this attitude as it gave them less to do. My treatment consisted of two injections of insulin each day and a visit from the specialist once a week. I understand that insulin is only used for diabetes and not deaf ears!

Most of the nurses were volunteers for the duration of the war and came from well-to-do Florentine families. The one who had most to do with me was called Traxler Camerana, and she brought me flowers for the room and pre-war English books and magazines for me to read. Her mother was Swiss and her father Italian and I think she hated the war and the Fascists, but never in her talks to me was she disloyal to her country. She could speak French and German as easily as Italian, and usually we talked in a mixture of the first two languages so that the carabinieri outside my door would not know what was being discussed. Her husband was in the Navy and she had two pretty children whom she brought to the hospital to see me. My German improved considerably during the month and I could speak quite fluently, if a little ungrammatically, at the end. She told me of her home, her love for peace, and the English visitors to Florence before the war and a hundred and one anecdotes about life in wartime Florence, such as her difficulties with rationing and the black market, or a description of a cocktail party or a holiday by the sea. In fact she opened the window to the outside world a little and helped me to keep my sanity. She certainly reversed some of my opinions of the Italians as a race. "I am so sorry," she said, "that I cannot help you any more, for I have my children and my home to think of." I hope that she was not penalised when I eventually escaped. She certainly did not deserve to be.

The wing where I was had rooms all about the same size, two on each side of the corridor. In addition there was a sitting-room and a balcony where I was allowed to sit in the morning. This balcony looked on to the main road outside the hospital, and this bird's-eye view of life outside was a constant attraction to me. The room next door to me was occupied by a Black Shirt lieutenant who had been wounded in Russia, and whom I rarely saw. On the other side of the corridor one room was empty and the second occupied by two Jugoslav generals who had been captured when their country was overrun. One had had an operation on his eye and the other on his ear, and both were at least sixty years old. We used to meet on the balcony every morning and they were cheery souls who disliked the Italians intensely. We got on quite well speaking German, and their tales were the usual hard-luck stories which every prisoner of war has and which can always be produced on demand. While I was in hospital, one of them had a letter to say that his whole family, wife and three children, had been shot by the Germans because there had been sabotage on the railway near the village where they lived. Poor old soul, he grew ten years older overnight; everything that he had been living for had suddenly been cut away from under his feet.

One day I saw a sight that I shall never forget, whilst sunning myself on the balcony. I remember reading a very similar description of the Italian Army by Ernest Hemingway which referred to the 1914–1918 war.

I could hear shouting and singing coming from some dis-

tance away, and it was not till a ragged band of men came
marching along the main road towards Florence that I realised that this was an Italian battalion on its way to the city
to take part in a local feast day celebration. There were no
officers to be seen at the head of the column, which was led
by senior N.C.O.s on bicycles. Some of the men carried
their rifles one way and some another, their uniforms were
shoddy and their equipment badly-fitting. A few even fell
out to talk to a passer-by, and then doubled up to take their
places in the column after they had finished their chats.
Their singing was confined to individuals trying to be ten-
ors and giving their own renderings, all different, of the
better-known operatic arias. The rabble, because that is its
best description, was divided into four lots, presumably
companies, and behind each minced three or four lieu-
tenants in tightly-fitting jack boots but no equipment except a Sam Browne belt to which a tiny pistol was attached
in its holster. The boots must have been extremely painful
from the expression on some of the officers' faces as they
gingerly marched along the road. Their sleek, oiled and
waved hair was draped over their ears and allowed to hang
over their collars at the back of their necks, while their hats
were worn at the jauntiest possible angle. The climax came
when a four-wheeled horse cab brought up the tail of the
column, in which a fat old major and his four captains sat
playing cards till the time came for them to take their place
at the head of their men and march triumphantly through
the main streets of Florence. It gave the Jugoslavs and me
the best laugh we had had for years, much to the annoyance of my carabinieri guard. The whole scene was so
pathetic in some ways, and yet so reminiscent of Mussolini

as the sawdust Cæsar. The Italian Army had not improved much, even with the help of Fascist discipline and all the shouting.

When I was in my room a carabiniere guard was on watch outside my door continuously, being relieved every eight hours. The door was kept locked. Every time I wanted to go to the lavatory I had to bang on it, when it was unlocked, and the carabiniere would walk with me to the lavatory just down the passage. When I sat on the verandah he came too, and the prospects of getting away did not seem very bright. Luckily the prison camp had not warned the hospital that I had escaped before and was considered "dangerous" or otherwise they would have taken rather more stringent precautions. Six months later, in England, I heard that the wretched Commandant of the prison camp was sent to the Russian front for not having warned the hospital!

Outside my window was a seventy-foot drop to the court-yard below and no handy drain pipes to slide down. The old device of knotted sheets for a rope could not be used because of their rottenness and the fact that the number I would require was many more than I could raise. However, there was a decorative moulding about four feet below my window, which ran all the way round the outside of the building. The top of the moulding was in the form of a slightly sloping ledge about six inches wide, and I thought it might be just wide enough to use.

Gradually my plan evolved. I would get out of my window and move along the ledge, past the Italian officer's bedroom window, round a corner of the building and then in at one of the lavatory windows. (I could easily make

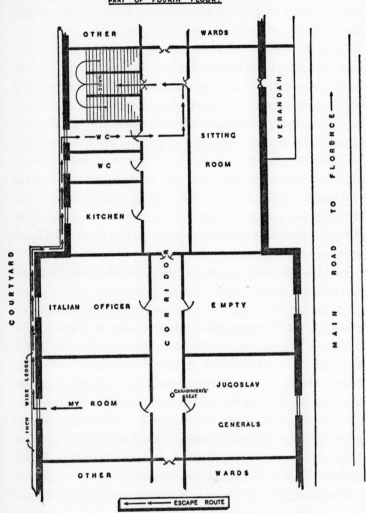

FLORENCE MILITARY HOSPITAL
PART OF FOURTH FLOOR.

OTHER   WARDS

DOWN

WC

WC

KITCHEN

SITTING

ROOM

VERANDAH

CORRIDOR

ITALIAN OFFICER   EMPTY

COURTYARD

6 INCH WIDE LEDGE

MY ROOM   CARABINIERIS'
SEAT

JUGOSLAV

GENERALS

OTHER   WARDS

MAIN ROAD. TO FLORENCE

←— ←— ESCAPE ROUTE

143

sure it was open by going to the lavatory about midnight.)
I would then go through the lavatory door, which I would
also leave open, and then down the stairs which were in a
well of their own and separated by doors from all landings. The snag was that I could not very well open the door
leading down the stairs when I went to the lavatory, but I
hoped that over a course of days I would be lucky one
night and find that it had been left open. The carabiniere
always sat in his chair facing my door and he would be most
unlikely to hear me flit in stockinged feet between the
already-opened lavatory and the stairway doors. Having
reached the ground floor I would jump out through a window into the courtyard, and circling round the building to
the right I could quite easily get on to the main road leading down into Florence.

I had been in the hospital a fortnight when my plan had
crystallised. About then a Flight-Sergeant Cox came into
my room for three days with tonsilitis. He was working as
a batman at the Generals' Prison Camp at Fiesole, just
outside Florence, having been captured when Air Vice-
Marshal Boyd was landed by mistake in Sicily instead of
Malta. He gave me all their news. He told me how Air
Marshal Boyd spent his whole time doing carpentry, how
General Gambier-Parry was a very able sketcher and
artist, and how General Younghusband was a most successful gardener within the limited area which was available.
General Carton de Wiart was the only one he could not
understand, but "he has only one arm, one eye, and a V.C.,
so that must explain a lot." I agreed.

At the time I thought it was just possible that he was a
stooge and so I did not tell him of my intentions. It was a

welcome respite, however, to be able to talk in English again.

As soon as Cox had gone back to Campo 12 at Fiesole, I started my midnight visits to the lavatory, but it wasn't until ten days later, on the evening of June 13th, 1942, that the door leading down the stairway was left open. June 13th was St. Anthony's Day, which I felt was a good omen for my adventure.

I decided to start about 3 a.m. and aimed at being on the main road by 4 a.m. This would give me two hours to walk into Florence and get an early train to Milan. In planning for our escape from Campo 27 I had remembered that an express train for Milan was due to leave at 6 a.m., and that was the one I hoped to catch.

I dressed as silently as possible, putting one shoe in each trouser pocket where they would not be in my way, and at 3 a.m., in my stockinged feet, I swung my legs over into the darkness and found the ledge with my toes. Holding on to the shutter outside window with one hand I started to move sideways to the left, flattening myself against the wall as much as possible. I had not gone more than a few steps when an attack of giddiness seized me, and I quickly went back, just managing to clutch on to my shutter again. My knees were shaking and teeth chattering with excitement as I climbed back into my bedroom.

Ten minutes went by while I recovered my breath and my nerve. An occasional grunt came through the door from the carabiniere or a squeak from his chair as his shifted his seat, but otherwise the night was silent. My imagination kept telling me that I might slip off the ledge, or it might crumble under my weight. But I knew I must do it. This was my chance; I might never get another one.

Once again I tiptoed to the window and without looking downwards, levered myself out and slowly slithered my feet down the wall on to the ledge. This time I was not going to get back into the room and to make sure of it, I swung the outside shutters across the window, and I heard a click from the latch on the inside.

I had always meant to do this to keep the Italians guessing how I had got out, but on my first try I had forgotten all about it in my excitement. I had bought some particularly obnoxious and sticky hair oil whilst in the hospital, and I had used this to lubricate all the hinges and catches on the shutters and on the lavatory door, to stop any squeaks.

There was no going back now. I held on to the closed shutter with my right hand and slid as far as I could along the ledge. My left hand could not reach the shutter over the next window but I forced myself on and inch by inch moved along the ledge. I wanted to press against the rough wall as tightly as possible, but if I did this it made a scraping noise which might alarm some wakeful patient.

After six feet with nothing to hang on to, I reached the next lot of shutters and, using them as hand holds, quickly passed under the window. I then came to the worst part of the ledge, where it went round the corner of the building out of reach of all shutters. Again I had to leave go with my right hand and move spread-eagled to the corner. Here the fingertips of my left hand were able to follow the wall around and give slightly more security. At the same moment the ledge under my left foot suddenly felt loose, and I had visions of the whole corner of the building breaking away. All at once my giddiness returned and I felt sweat slowly trickling down the side of my nose. My knees shook, but I held them still by pressing against the wall, while I gingerly transferred my weight to my other foot and felt around with my left toe to see what was loose. Something was very wobbly right on the corner and looking down I could just see that the cement surface was quite free and if dislodged, a three-foot length would crash into the court-yard below. The moulding underneath the surface felt solid enough. It made a gritting noise as it wobbled and felt very insecure, but I slowly worked my way round the corner and then along a short length of wall to another corner, which was an inside one and much easier. A few more yards and I was under the lavatory window.

I heaved myself up and dropped on to the lavatory floor where I stood for a minute or two to get my breath. Never have I felt so relieved as I did when I had finished that awful traverse along the face of the building in pitch dark-ness. Never do I want to do anything like it again. It might have been child's play to an expert mountaineer, but I was not one.

Cautiously peering round the corner of the lavatory door I saw the carabiniere awake and looking disconsolately at the ground in front of his chair. I saw that, if I crossed the passage to the other side before moving along opposite the doorway to the stairs, he could not see me if he looked up. All went well and soon I was standing opposite to the door-way leading down the stairs. There was not enough room for me to get through and I prayed and hoped that it would not squeak when I opened it a further few inches. The door opened without a murmur and, like a flash, I passed down the stairs without the carabiniere knowing what was happening. I would have a clear five hours' start till about 8 a.m. when I was called, and by that time I hoped to be well on the way to Milan. In case the carabiniere put his head inside my room during the remainder of the night, I had rolled up a great coat to look like me in bed, and I was confident it would pass all right for any casual look.

Creeping down the stairs I arrived at the bottom, and dropped into the courtyard through an open window on the ground floor. I rather misjudged the height because I landed on the paving stones on all fours and severely strained my wrist in the process. I crept round the outside of the hospital and then through an allotment and so came to the wall bordering the main road where I put on my shoes. I also pulled out a brown paper parcel from my trouser seat, which I planned to carry instead of a bag to give me the necessary *raison d'être*. It was five minutes to four, and at four o'clock precisely I swung over the wall and started to walk down the main road towards Florence.

Chapter XII

GERMAN SEAMAN

THIS TIME I had decided to wear no outer insignia to suggest that I was a German. I did not in fact have any papers with me as it would have been too risky to bring them into hospital. Only if I was challenged would I say I was a German, and then only if I had to say more than a word or two in Italian. By 5 a.m. I had reached the centre of Florence and had to ask my way to the station which I reached about twenty minutes later. To my relief I found that there was a 6 a.m. to Milan, but decided to wander round the station till about ten minutes to six before buying my ticket. By that time there would be a good-sized queue and this would give the booking-clerk less time to look at me closely.

Florence station is modern, and puts ours to shame by its cleanliness and neat layout. I looked round for a bench where I feigned sleep to avoid complications in talking. When the time came I pulled out my money and rose to join the queue for tickets. Unfortunately my 500 lire note was slightly mutilated because it had been hidden up the tubular leg of an iron bedstead at Campo 27 and little holes had been torn in it. Eventually my turn came and I said my usual *"terzo Milano,"* at the same time pushing over the note. To my horror the official started turning the note over and over, examining it against the light, and, after what seemed hours, asked me if I had another. I replied with a shake of the head and a monosyllabic mumbled "no." However, with a shrug of his shoulders he pushed the ticket and change towards me. Cold sweat had started on my brow and the palms of my hands were decidedly damp as I walked away.

The express from Rome came in ten minutes late, and was very full. As soon as it came to a halt the crowd surged forward, myself included, and we fought for places on the steps leading up to the carriages. Putting my head down I got aboard after giving a kick on the shins to a man on my left who had tried to pull me back to get in himself. At last we all crammed into the corridor where I stood in the corner near the lavatory, chin on chest, pretending to doze. I kept my ticket in my hand and whenever the collector passed up and down the train, which happened frequently, he just took the ticket out of my hand, punched it and put it back without apparently waking me up.

A lot of people got out at Bologna and I was glad to find a seat to myself in a compartment, as I would need all my energy when I reached the frontier. Unfortunately no "cistina" lunches were being sold on the stations, rations in Italy being much shorter now than when I had travelled to Milan six months earlier.

On one occasion when the ticket-collector came round he had two railway police behind him, and they took a good look at me when punching the ticket. He took the ticket out into the corridor and started examining it closely with his back to me. After a minute or two he returned it and passed on to the next person. Scare over! Apparently they had a special key which fitted the ticket exactly for detecting forgeries. In all my travels on the railway I always saw hundreds of carabinieri, railway policemen and ordinary railway officials but they were always more concerned with the traveller who had no ticket. As long as you had a bona-fide ticket they did not seem to worry.

I managed to avoid all conversation by pretending to sleep in my corner, and at 11 a.m. we pulled into Milan Central Station. My plan was to hang about the station till about 4:30 p.m. and then take a train to Varese, as I thought Como might be watched by now. The frontier was only thirteen kilometres from Varese at Porto Cerisio on the edge of Lago Lugano. If I arrived at Varese about dusk I would then walk to within two kilometres of Porto Cerisio and then strike up the hill and with a bit of luck might be in Switzerland within twenty-four hours of getting away from Florence.

The waiting-room was much emptier this time and I killed time by wandering round the station. I bought my ticket, just in case anybody asked me what I was doing and got a return this time to make my travelling to a frontier town more plausible. "*Terzo Varese andate e riturno,*" accompanied by a fifty lire note produced my ticket without any questions being asked. I was always a little self-conscious about my dress, but it never seemed to excite any suspicions. Luckily it was fairly cool at that date and the roll-neck pullover did not look too out of place.

I had a cup of *caffè al latte* for my lunch, and buying a few papers took them to the waiting-room for a four-hour wait till my train, which left at 4:37. I saw in the paper that a German ship had been sunk in the Mediterranean and the survivors landed at Genoa. This might be a useful story if ever I was stopped, and my navy blue sweater would help. I could always pretend I was taking a short holiday before going on to Germany.

The journey to Varese by electric train was without incident and I arrived at about 6:15 p.m., just when it was beginning to get dark. My half ticket was taken without any questions being asked, and I went out into the town. My plan was to strike off along the road which led roughly in the right direction and hope it brought me to a signpost which would put me on my way. I walked right through the centre of the town and past groups of men and women gossiping on the pavements and sitting at open air cafés; but they seemed to be far more interested in their own conversations than in me, so I passed through unmolested.

A crossroad on the north side of the town put me on the right road and told me I had twelve kilometres to Porto Cerisio. By this time it was dark and the sky was overcast, but a moon shone behind the clouds for the first half of the night. The road twisted and turned in all directions but always seemed to be flanked by small fields, high walls or precipitous mountainsides. It was no country to choose one's own route until much closer to the frontier. The road seemed to be interminable. My month in hospital without exercise had not helped and my muscles were very soft. I passed through one or two tiny villages and eventually came to the three kilometre stone from Porto Cerisio, where I could see Lago Lugano with searchlights playing on the water. By this time it was 10 p.m. and I struck up the hillside through a wood which flanked the road at this point. Thorn bushes seemed to reach out and grab me with every step I took and made progress very slow and painful. It was dark in the wood and I was forced to move so slowly that, having gone about two hundred yards, I decided to wait until morning when I would be able to avoid some of the worst hazards. Feeling thirsty, tired and cold, I curled myself up in some dead leaves and went to sleep. The cold woke me up about an hour before dawn, and after rubbing my stiff muscles back to life I crawled up the hill trying to avoid the demon thorn bushes. After half an hour, I saw I was coming to the top of the ridge. Suddenly, outlined against the morning sky, I saw a sentry box with a tall row of barbed wire behind it. I immediately dropped to the ground and saw that the sentry boxes were spaced about fifty yards apart all along the top of the hill. Just round the corner, and lower down, I could see what looked like a cemetery. This was really too much! My map did not show the frontier in any great detail but I had never expected to find it so close to the main road and so well guarded. In a minor panic I slithered back down the hill up which I had just crawled, and wondered what to do next. I was really flabbergasted, having hoped that this piece of the frontier would not have been more difficult than the part near Chiasso that I had seen six months before. Rightly or wrongly I decided to lie up where I was for the rest of that day, and then to walk back to Varese and on to Como that night. I would then try to get over a piece of frontier that I knew.

Later on, in Switzerland, I found a large-scale map of where I had been, and the frontier could not have been there at all and was at least another two kilometres farther on. To this day I do not know what I had stumbled into, and can only suppose that it was some kind of military dump that was being extra well guarded. I had not bargained for that sort of bad luck. To make matters worse it rained cats and dogs all that day, and I was soaked to the skin. I had to remain perfectly still so as not to attract attention and I don't think I have ever been so cold in all my life. My teeth kept up a permanent chatter and the feeling went out of my hands and feet after an hour or two. Slowly the time went by and at last it was dark enough to allow me to walk down to the main road and get my circulation going once more. It was about twenty miles to Como and I thought I could arrive in its vicinity by midnight.

It was lovely to be warm again and my clothes soon dried out, but I was certainly not out of the wood yet. I passed through Varese for the second time about 9 p.m., and found the Como road without difficulty. I began to feel extraordinarily tired and my brown Italian shoes were working up beautiful blisters on my heels which did not help progress. To my left I could see the outline of hills and over them I knew lay Switzerland, my dream country for over a year past. The road seemed never ending and I began to curse myself for having decided to walk all the way round to Como before trying again. If I had had a more accurate map of the frontier I would have gone across country but it was too risky on my own and would have been more guesswork than map reading.

I don't know what possessed me but I went on walking after midnight, always a dangerous thing to do. At about 1 a.m., while passing through the little village of Ogliate, I was challenged. My spirits fell as I went up to the man who proved to be a Maresciallo of the Bersaglieri (equivalent of R.S.M.—Regimental Sergeant-Major). He asked me for my papers. I went into a long explanation of who I was and brought out my newspaper to prove it, but all I could get out of him was that I would have to go in "*dentro*" (inside) for the night. The last card I had to play was to knock him on the head, seize his bicycle and make a run for it, but before this I tried my last piece of bluff. I told him that if the German Consular authorities in Como did not see me by 8 a.m. in the morning, there would be trouble for anyone who had held me. I said this with much gusto and repeated myself several times. With much head-shaking and more muttering of "*dentro*" he said I could go on this time, but it was most irregular and I must not do it again. My luck was holding out, but that scare had brought me to my senses and I did not make such a stupid mistake again. I went on through the village and slept in a ditch about one kilometre along the road till about 4:30, when I started to walk again. I passed through another village and had a dirty look from a carabiniere on duty, but soon after this I discovered a little wood near the road that would do as shelter for the day. Creeping in under some under-growth, I curled up and went to sleep, mentally and physi-cally exhausted, but thankful that I was still a free man.

I woke up at 11 a.m. to the sound of woodcutting and children playing about a hundred and fifty yards away in my wood. Children and dogs were my worst enemies that day, but luckily none came near enough to find me, though it had the effect of keeping me mentally alert and awake all the time. I was now getting very hungry and thirsty and my blistered feet did not help my physical condition. How-ever, I knew that I was now within a few miles of freedom and that, given a bit of luck and provided I did not make a fool of myself, I would have a good chance of succeeding. It was my gamble against at least another six months in prison, if not for the whole war. I was playing for uncomfortably high stakes. I suppose the chances of getting out of a prison camp are at least a hundred-to-one against. In Italy at this time, one's chances of getting to the frontier area having got out of camp were about twenty-to-one against—provided one did not do anything too stupid. Having got to within five miles of the frontier the chances of getting over would be about evens. I had now, for the second time in six months, arrived within five miles of the frontier, so I considered my chances were really good but did not mean to take any risks.

That day, thank goodness, was dry; for I don't think I could have stood another soaking. When dusk came I started on what I hoped would be my last lap. The road began to climb and, in a series of gentle turns, I went on upwards for the first three hours. The country was getting very hilly and the mountains to the north seemed to tower to endless heights above me. An occasional car swept by and I would shield my face from the lights and try and keep in the shadows on the sides of the road. Houses were built on either side and became more frequent. They were obviously summer villas for rich businessmen from Milan, and must have been delightful with an endless view stretching out over the Lombardy plain.

A few men passed me going the other way and once two or three soldiers went by, but they had no eyes for me and I certainly had none for them. At last my road started to wend its way down the hillside and, far below, I could see some lights with a lake beyond. At the time I assumed they must be Como, but I discovered later that it was the goods yard at Chiasso, on the frontier, at which I was now looking.

Eventually at about 11 p.m. I came to a road junction and turned left towards the lights thinking that it would lead me to Como through which I should have to pass before reaching the frontier area at Chiasso. In fact, of course, my road had by-passed Como, and I had just joined the Como-Chiasso road where I had been caught before. I suppose I should have recognised it, but it looked very different by night and distances were deceptive.

I walked on down the hill to Chiasso and did not realise my mistake until suddenly I saw the frontier barrier right across the road and not two hundred yards away from me. I nearly had a fit on the spot. Trying not to hurry myself, I retraced my steps to the outskirts of Chiasso, and, not wishing to be caught on the roads again after hours, I decided to sleep in a culvert under the road until about 4:30 a.m., when I would go back towards Como for about a mile and then strike up the hill. My culvert could not have been more than a few hundred yards from the frontier, but it was a case of safety first at this stage. Unfortunately it was not entirely dry and an evil-smelling stream of dirty black water trickled down the middle. I had an uncomfortable, worrying five hours perched on some flat stones which remained dry at one side of the stream.

At last 4:30 a.m. crept round on my watch and, making sure that nobody saw me coming out of the culvert, I started walking back down the road. In ten minutes I found a convenient turning off and soon I was following a small footpath that led up the hillside and in approximately the right general direction. I would be much too early for any woodcutters going to work, and my only worry was the possibility of frontier guards coming back from duty along my track. However, I reasoned to myself that the relief guard would surely have to use my track to go out, and I could not imagine a changeover much before 6:30 a.m. With any luck my path would be all right for at least an hour, and after that I must keep well clear of all tracks. My progress along the path was five times as quick as it would have been across country, as by now I was climbing nearly vertical slopes with thick thorny undergrowth on either side.

At 6 a.m. I decided to leave the track and started climbing straight up the hill. I was now about two thousand feet above the valley. I could see Chiasso quite plainly with its long goods sidings, and an obvious fence at right angles through the middle which was the frontier.

I decided to climb for about another hour and then to start moving very slowly along the hillside till I sighted the frontier. I would then lie up all day watching the sentries, and try to get over that night.

I thrust my way up the mountainside and swept aside the bushes that tried to hold me back; what did a few scratches matter now? Soon I came to a belt of pine trees, and walking through them was a great relief after the thorn scrub lower down. I came out of the pine trees and went on upwards through hazel plantations and every sort of mountain shrub, which all grew in profusion everywhere. At last I thought I was high enough and I started to move cautiously along the hillside in the direction where I knew the frontier to be. I had not been going more than half an hour, when, just across a little valley and not more than four hundred yards away, I saw a sentry box amongst the trees. I dropped down on one knee and could pick out one or two more and the line of fence poles behind. The little valley between me and the frontier was quite bare and open and the fence and sentry boxes were a few yards inside the wood beyond. I found a comfortable hole full of dead leaves in which I could sleep and from which I could watch the frontier. I had a very welcome meal of blueberries, which grew all around, and after watching the frontier for an hour or two fell asleep.

About half a mile up on my left hand, and just about where the frontier ought to be, I could see a red roof. I assumed this to be one of the posts which housed the relief sentries, and occasionally I could see one wandering along the wire. They changed over every even hour. The sentry boxes were about two hundred yards apart, which was not too bad, and I carefully marked down the route I should take that night in order to bring me out exactly between two boxes.

At last darkness fell and, although I felt like going bald-headed at it, I had decided to play safe and try to cross at 11 p.m. I would allow an hour to crawl the four hundred yards and that would give me at least another hour before there was any more large movement of sentries to and fro. The sentries on that frontier were not over-keen on wandering about by day, so with any luck they would be even less alert at night. A light rain started to fall about 10 p.m. and I cheered inwardly to myself. No Italian sentry would wander about in the rain unless given a direct order by an officer!

I crawled slowly through the undergrowth and across the open patch at the bottom of the valley. I did not make much noise, but to my ears I sounded like a bull charging around. The rain pattering on the leaves made all the difference as it blanketed my sounds from the sentries. I could just hear one singing away to himself in his box, little suspecting that a British officer was at that very moment within a hundred yards of his post.

By 11 p.m. I had reached the path used by the sentries and just over the other side the frontier wire was stretched. I saw that it was a fairly formidable obstacle. It was made of diamond mesh wire of fairly heavy gauge and was constructed all in one piece and at least twelve feet high. Poles in the form of an inverted V suspended the wire from its apex, and all along the top, bells were hung. The slightest touch on the wire would start them clanging. The problem was how to get over, through, or under. No branches overhung the wire anywhere near and as I had no pliers my only alternative was to try to burrow a way underneath. I could have risked the bells and climbed over the top but it might have gone wrong and was not worth it if I could find another way.

The bottom of the fence was pegged every six inches with eighteen-inch wooden stakes, but luckily the soil in the wood was mostly leaf mould, and the stakes pulled up easily without shaking the fence. I had soon freed about a three-foot length, pausing between each stake to listen for any footsteps on the path.

All was quiet. The sentry on my left was still crooning

away to himself about his *"Mama mia,"* but I could hear nothing from the one on my right. The rain came down a little harder now, and a damp moist smell came up from the disturbed earth when I started to scrape it away with my hands. It reminded me of sheltering from the rain in an English wood in autumn after a dry summer. It was a musty clean smell quite different from the usual pungent Italian aromas.

I slowly scraped away, using one of the stakes to loosen the earth, and then removing it with my hands.

After I had been going about ten minutes there was quite a respectable hole and I tried to squeeze underneath the wire but there was too small a gap and I became stuck with one shoulder and one arm in Switzerland and the rest of me in Italy.

Several things then happened at once. The bell above me gave a very small tinkle, a branch crashed down nearby, the sentry stopped singing and the noise of shunting goods wagons in Chiasso suddenly became very loud due to a change in the wind.

I prayed that the sentries would stay where they were, whilst I slowly pushed myself back into Italy. The hole would have to be bigger.

After a few very long seconds I was clear and I crawled back over the track and lay in a bush for a few minutes. If the sentry had heard anything he would surely come along and inspect the wire at once.

My luck was in and after five minutes' complete silence except for the rain on the leaves, and the noise of the shunting, I crawled back across the track once more. On this occasion I was not going to be stuck under the wire, and worked away for ten minutes before the gap was big enough. My hands reached through to Switzerland, this time much farther, and I was able to grasp a tree root and draw myself through without shaking the fence above me.

Chapter XIII

SWITZERLAND, JUNE 1942

I·WAS NOW in Switzerland and free! My hunger, tiredness and sore feet were all forgotten in my elation and satisfaction. Walking erect, and no longer afraid of making a noise, I went a few hundred yards away from the line of the wire and then started down the hill with the lights of Chiasso to guide me. I then struck the most enormous patch of thorn bushes and only after about half an hour of struggling did I manage to free myself. As a result I decided to sleep the rest of the night on the hillside and to walk down in the morning when I could see where I was going.

I curled up under a large tree that kept off most of the rain, and slept till about 4 a.m. when I woke to see the eastern sky just starting to lighten. Overhead the clouds had gone, making visibility much better, and gradually I began to see where I was. By 5 a.m. I was on my way and I soon struck a path which I followed till it eventually brought me on to a road that led down into Chiasso. The atmosphere was altogether different, the people just stirring at the backs of their houses looked clean and hospitable and the occasional Swiss sign reassured me that the almost unbelievable had come true, and that I had actually arrived in a neutral country.

I was soon walking through the outskirts of the town

and, on reaching the main square, I sat down on a bench while deciding what to do next. I knew that in theory all I had to do was to present myself to the first Swiss policeman, and that he would take care of the rest and see that I was taken to the nearest Consulate. We had heard in the prison camp that it was still possible to get back from Switzerland to England, in spite of Vichy France and Spain being in the way. My reasoning had become ultra-cautious by now and I said to myself that if I could get to the British Embassy in Berne without the Swiss knowing, I might be in an even stronger position to be sent back to England. After all, if I could travel through Italy without being spotted, I ought to be able to do so easily enough in peaceful Switzerland. Anyway, I would go to the station and see if I could change my Italian money for Swiss. Without Swiss money I could do nothing. I would then try to buy a ticket to Berne and then if there was time I would go out and have a shave and some breakfast.

I found the station and the *bureau de change,* and received twenty-five Swiss francs in exchange for about four hundred lire. So far so good. I next bought a ticket, speaking German this time, and to my surprise out came my third class ticket to Berne. It was almost too good to be true and could not last. It didn't!

I had an hour to spare before the next train went and was just walking out of the station when a Swiss policeman politely asked me who I was. The game was up, and so I told him in German that I was a British officer escaped from Italy and I was just going out to have a shave before taking the 7:15 a.m. train to Berne. This took his breath away a bit, and all he could mutter was, "It is most irregular." I agreed with him and said that I did not suppose it happened every day, but then I was lucky and would he mind telling me the way to the nearest barber?

By this time he had come to his senses and told me he did not believe a word that I had said and that I was probably a German spy. Anyway, I would have to come down to the frontier post for interrogation by his boss. Frontier posts in Chiasso seemed to have a fatal attraction for me, but I hoped this one would be a little more hospitable. I went with the policeman to the post and there, not twenty yards away, was the Italian equivalent which had housed me only six months before. I was searched and questioned and after a little telephoning I was told that the H.Q. at Bellinzona wanted to check up on me and that I should be going there in a few hours. All the officials were most polite and after I had told them that I had not washed, eaten or slept for three days, immediately sent for some breakfast and a barber.

A huge bowl of coffee soon slipped down, accompanied by several crisp, warm rolls spread with delicious butter and jam. My morale was picking up with every mouthful and after a wash and a shave I felt like a million dollars. Everything was wonderful, the countryside clean and well cared for, with happy, smiling people who looked so different from their neighbours across the frontier. I wore rose-tinted spectacles that day.

After breakfast we walked to the station and I was soon on my way to Bellinzona, accompanied by a policeman. A sudden weariness overcame me on the train and I slept all the way until I was nudged to get out when we walked through the town to the police H.Q.

I was led in front of the Chief of Police, and the first question he asked me was why I had not given myself up instead of trying to go to Berne direct. I told him that I was frightened of the delay and red tape that might prevent me getting to Berne quickly. I reminded him that I had been with Italians for a year and a half where "*domani*" or "to-morrow" was the watchword and everything could wait. This riled him a little, and he sharply reminded me that I was now in Switzerland and not Italy. Anyhow it had the desired effect because I was in Berne by 7 p.m. that night. Having rebuked me, he asked me if I would like anything to eat and I told him I would like a really large steak with fried potatoes and half a litre of beer. Before the meal I went to wash my hands and had the shock of my life when I saw my face in the glass. I looked quite frightful with a thin, pinched face and weary eyes sunk into the cheekbones. I weighed myself the next day in Berne and found that I was forty pounds under my normal weight.

That meal was one of the best and most satisfying I have ever eaten, and I don't think the old Chief of Police had ever seen anyone eat so hungrily. His eyes nearly popped out of his head as he saw it all disappearing down my throat, and we parted on the best of terms when the time came to catch the train to Berne. I dozed on and off all the way, but we passed through the most lovely scenery imaginable, and I was so enthralled with the view that only occasionally did my eyelids take control and close over my eyes for half an hour or so. It was evening when we drew into Berne station.

We took a taxi to a military H.Q. and the things that struck me most were the lighted shop windows and the enormous variety of goods for sale everywhere. It was quite a revelation and helped me to become a little more normal and a little less affected by my period in prison. We arrived at a big stone building and I was interviewed by a charming young officer who said that I would be questioned in the morning, but that I would have to spend to-night in the refugees' hostel. He took me there and I found a babel of voices speaking every tongue from all over Europe. Little Switzerland was a haven for oppressed people and the Swiss were in the embarrassing situation of entertaining thousands of penniless refugees without a country, and who for humanitarian reasons alone could not be turned back.

The little Swiss officer left me after I had found a bed, and rather disconsolately I lay on my back wondering what to do next. Visions of a bath and food at the best restaurant in Berne faded before the rather hospital-like rugged simplicity of the refugees' hostel. Outside, guards patrolled all round the building and I began to feel a little depressed.

I was reprieved quicker than I expected because two hours later the same officer came back, and said that I could stay in an hotel for the night if I promised not to try and communicate with my Embassy. I readily agreed and we walked round to it by the way of his flat, where I picked up some clothes which he lent me till I could get some others, as he thought I would be a little uncomfortable in my battledress trousers and now dirty roll-neck pullover in a big Berne hotel. This was very kind of him and most thoughtful. I was shown my room by the hotel manager, who became most effusive as soon as he knew who I was. In the luxury of a steaming hot bath, I lay back and forgot all my worries. It was my first for fifteen months and a wonderful relaxation after my long journey.

The next day I was questioned and apparently I satisfied them that my story was bona fide. The following fortnight in Switzerland was almost like a fairy tale. Cocktail parties, dinners, dances, sailing and swimming. I had my first real holiday of the war and I don't think I let the grass grow under my feet. The feeling of freedom was so pleasant and the kindly, hospitable people and the cleanliness of the streets contrasted vividly with wartime Italy.

I then moved down to Geneva, which was the start of my next lap. Now, of course, it was a very different matter because instead of having to work out my own route, provide myself with clothes, money, etc., it was all done for me.

My grey suit was chosen for its continental style and cut and had wide trousers, padded shoulders and patch pockets. A little dark blue beret and an attaché case completed my outfit for my new rôle of a Czechoslovak refugee.

I joined up with two R.A.F. sergeant-pilots who had walked all the way to Switzerland from northern France, and we three were to travel together to Marseilles. We all lived in an unobtrusive hotel in Geneva, waiting for the word to start us once more on our adventures. I went for long walks round the city each day, including seeing over that expensive white elephant, the Palace of the League of Nations. Then I used to bathe and go out for sails on the lake. In the evening my still insatiable hunger would get the better of me and I would go to the open-air lakeside restaurants for an exquisite meal, which of course was to prove far better than any I was able to get in London a few weeks later. Meals at restaurants were rationed and no more than three meal coupons could be expended at any one restaurant for a single meal. As I had been given a whole month's coupons, and I knew I was only going to be there about another week, I used to have hors d'œuvres and fish at one restaurant, and then move along to the next and finish off the meal. I was still about two stone under weight and my appetite always appeared to demand more.

At last our moment came and about an hour before dawn one morning a car picked us up at our hotel and drove us rapidly to the place where we were going to cross the frontier. A guide led the way through a churchyard and along the edge of a wood which had a small stream running through it. An occasional Swiss soldier could be seen on frontier duty, but a mumbled password from our guide was sufficient to make the sentry turn away and carry on along his beat. I am sure we were not the only ones to use that crossing point, and it was clear that the Swiss authorities did not know what was going on.

Our guide pointed out our route and with a "Good luck" and a handshake he left us alone. After we had taken off our shoes we stepped gingerly across the stream, which was only about nine inches deep, and climbed up the farther bank. We then had to cross a small field and go through a gate on to a road. I knew we had to move about a hundred yards along this road when Simon, our next guide, would come out from behind a hedge with a bicycle on his left side. I saw the bit of hedge that had been described to me, but to my dismay no Simon appeared. The two R.A.F. sergeants, who had not been given the instructions, wanted to know if I had remembered the right way and couldn't it have been in the opposite direction. Just when we were looking a bit sheepish at one another, Simon came bicycling up the road and said, in a very casual tone, he was sorry he was late.

We then walked to his house where Madame Simon produced the biggest and best omelet I have ever seen or tasted. It must have been made with a dozen eggs and about half a pound of butter. Not much starvation here, but no doubt it was all purchased on the black market.

After breakfast we cleaned ourselves up and awaited our next guide who took us to the other side of the town and nearer to the railway station from which we were to catch the night train to Marseilles. Henri appeared at nine o'clock and he led us round by a carefully chosen route to his house. He knew exactly when all the patrols went by, and by which route. A little palm-greasing here and there and our route seemed as safe as walking through Hyde Park.

We had another excellent meal with Henri and passed the rest of the day in his house. We were rather bored but heard many tales of the difficulties and dangers of a patriot in France at this time. German Gestapo men in plain clothes were everywhere and nobody knew who was friend or foe. Suddenly someone would disappear and never be heard of again, except six months or perhaps a year later a small box containing ashes arrived by post for his relations.

With our tickets already in our hands, we walked a few hundred yards to the station and went straight into the buffet to await the arrival of the train. The Gestapo were wandering around the platform and occasionally checked up on papers. Apparently they never came into the buffet. As soon as the train came in, Georges, our new guide, called

us on to the platform and we ran for a carriage door. Soon
we were on board and sitting in opposite corners of the
same compartment pretending not to recognise each other.
Dumbness was the order of the day and we spoke not a
word all that night on our way down the Rhone valley to
Marseilles, which we reached next morning at 7 a.m.

Marseilles was meant to have about thirty thousand police of one sort or another in it but it was such a large town
that any crook might well have hidden away in it for years
without discovery, which was a fact well known to every
wanted man in France. Georges led the way down the main
street from the station, past the hotel where the German-
Italian Commission was housed, and into a little café which
had opened early for the sale of ersatz coffee and rolls,
which were very welcome to us. Jean, our next guide, came
in a few minutes later and, after thanking Georges profusely, we were led off for quite a distance through the
streets.

No praise can be too high for these guides of the French
Resistance. They asked for no reward and they looked embarrassed when thanked; all they wanted was to do something towards the day when France would be liberated.
Each had his sector to work and did not know where the
next guide went. Only one master brain knew all the links
in the chain.

We walked through a very poor quarter and up the winding stairs of a dirty apartment house. This was not our final
goal and we collected our next guide, a young girl of about
twenty, who took us to a modern block of flats overlooking
the old harbour. A gendarme was standing outside the door,
but without faltering we went straight in and up the lift to

Madame Nouveau's flat, a luxurious apartment through which many an escaper like me passed during the course of the war. I believe I was number 123 to go through the flat and nothing could have been more hospitable than Madame during the ten days I spent there from July 2nd to 12th, 1942.

Her husband was up north on a job for the Resistance and Madame was carrying on in his absence. Six months later he was caught and put in Buchenwald Concentration Camp for the rest of the war. He had only been arrested on suspicion or otherwise he would have been executed. Luckily Madame Nouveau heard of her husband's arrest in time to go underground, and she remained undetected for two years until at last her hideaway in Haute-Savoie was overrun by the U.S. 7th Army. Before fleeing she had stripped her flat of everything from books to carpets and from ornaments to heavy oak chests-of-drawers. All her friends took what they could and promised to keep it for her till that glorious day, the day of Liberation.

When it did come and Madame returned, her friends brought everything back and she says she lost not a single tiny ornament or even a book. I revisited her flat in 1945 when my plane taking me to the Middle East broke down at Istres. This gave me an extra twenty-four hours, and I took the chance to hook a lift into Marseilles and found the flat I had known so well in 1942. With trepidation I knocked on the door and, to my enormous surprise and relief, saw Monsieur and Madame together in their flat, which looked exactly as I had remembered it in 1942. I soon had their news and I was told that I was the first of those whom they had helped during the war who had revisited them. Right royally did they welcome me once more, and once more all I could do was to thank them again and again for all they had done for poor wretches like me.

Squadron-Leader Whitney Straight, D.F.C., had come there a few days before we arrived. He had been shot down in northern France about a year before and had walked all the way to the Pyrenees, only to be caught by Vichy gendarmes and put in a prison camp in the Alpes-Maritimes. With others he escaped from this camp and as soon as he got out was escorted like us to Marseilles to await further instructions.

The resistance cell of which Monsieur Nouveau was, I believe, the leader, was highly organised and very efficient. They had direct wireless communication with England and all our instructions came that way. Apparently the Spanish route that had been used successfully for some time was very hot at the moment and they did not think it feasible. We were going out by a special method that had not been used for prisoners before, but had been employed for Polish refugees.

At last the day came for our departure and, in two parties, we made our way to the station and boarded a train for the west. We changed trains once at a small station, then at about 4 p.m. arrived at our destination about fifty miles from Marseilles and quite close to the sea. Our guides took us along different routes, but eventually we all met at our rendezvous in a small wood a few hundred yards from the Mediterranean. In addition to those of us that had come from Marseilles, two more parties of R.A.F. arrived at our wood before nightfall, to make a total of eight British with half a dozen French guides. We munched some sandwiches and drank coffee from thermoses and dozed off for a few hours' sleep before our next move which was not to be before eleven o'clock that night.

We were all in the highest spirits and all talked excitedly about what we would do when we arrived home, and we wondered how long it would take. Just as it was getting dark, a leading French politician and his wife turned up. They had travelled all the way from Paris to make our rendezvous and had been brought the last part of the way by guides just as we had been. He could talk English reasonably well and told us about his experiences at great length all the time we were with him. He was very interesting about German methods in France, but I always had the suspicion that his tales were told second-hand and were, for the most part, exaggerated. They would have gone down all right in England, where the ordinary person's idea of life on the Continent during the occupation years was pretty vague, but not to us who had just been in his country and in fact were still there! It always amazed me how the average Englishman thought that the whole population of Europe was either starving or collaborators or in a concentration camp or even sometimes all three. Except in the coastal areas, life was very much the same as it had always been in France, with the exception that most of the young men were prisoners of war or doing forced labour in Germany.

At 11 p.m. we all moved off in single file. The night was dark with no moon, and scudding clouds that alternately gave inky blackness or a feeble light that enabled us to see about a hundred yards. We wound our way in and out of enormous boulders going parallel to the seashore and a few hundred yards from it, and after about two miles' stumbling along this rocky labyrinth, we made our way down to the beach and walked along it for about another mile. The white, foamy edge of surf stood out in the darkness on our left and gave us a guide to walk by, while an occasional seaside villa on our right made us realise that the coast was inhabited and there might be many a slip 'twixt cup and lip. Lighthouses were flashing ahead and behind us and must have been about five miles apart on small promontories that protruded from either end of our beach.

When our guide judged us to be about half-way between the two lights he stopped and pulled out a torch, which had had a special blue filter over the glass. The time was now midnight and the ship which was coming to take us off, due at 1 a.m. on July 13th, would flash two long dashes of blue light which would be answered by three flashes from our torch. A rowing-boat would then come in and take us off.

Patiently we sat down and tried to keep warm while the hour went slowly by. A fine rain started that did not help and I think we were all wondering what on earth would happen if the boat failed to find us. We could not have hung around that beach until the next night, and there would have been an awful anti-climax and no little risk while we found hiding places for the day somewhere in the neighbourhood.

Our doubts and fears were laid at rest when, at 1 a.m. precisely, two faint blue flashes came out of the darkness in the bay and were answered by our signal. All we had to do now was to wait for the rowing-boat which might be twenty minutes coming in. Half an hour went by and still no sign of the boat. We gave some more flashes on our lamp, but these were not answered by the ship. What could have happened? Had we dreamt those blue flashes? However, we decided to give it another twenty minutes before we did anything more.

The twenty minutes went by and another twenty minutes as well. It was now ten-past two and still no sign of any rowing-boats. We just went on flashing while hoping for the best and giving our lamp as wide an arc as possible, in case the ship had drifted down-wind.

At half-past two there was still no sign and our guides began to look very worried. We were by now a very big party and would have been no easy problem for them. They would have to get us away by 3 a.m. if they were going to have a reasonable chance of finding somewhere for us to hide by daylight. My heart was sinking and I was trying to be cheerful and not depressed—I remember telling Whitney Straight that it was bound to be all right as 13 was my lucky number and to-day was July 13th. "Well, I hope you are right," he said, "I am not too happy myself."

The words were hardly out of his lips when a blue flash came from the sea and not more than a few hundred yards out. Soon we heard the padded noise made by muffled row-locks, and at 2:45 a.m. the rowing-boat beached. A midshipman in naval uniform was in the stern and a couple of husky A.B.s were at the oars. Apparently the off-shore wind and current had been very strong and, after making one abortive effort to row ashore, they had returned to the ship for another hand.

We piled aboard and pulled off after saying good-bye with many *au revoirs* to our brave guides. Two of us lent a hand at the oars and in ten minutes we sighted the outline of a small ship against the night sky, and had soon climbed up a scaling net helped by many willing hands on deck. We were then taken into the fo'c'stle and had enormous mugs of Navy cocoa, bread and jam and cheese thrust into our hands. It was wonderful to hear the cheery naval slang going on all round and English being talked again. Even while we sipped the boiling cocoa, the ship's engines started to murmur and we were heading out to sea away from our bay.

The Captain of the ship came in to speak to us and see who we were. He told us it was so nice to pick up Englishmen, as usually he had nothing but Poles. We asked him how on earth he managed to sail so close to an enemy shore with so small a ship, and he told us we would see how in the morning when we took a look round. A twinkle came into his eye, as he said, "You see, we look just like a peaceable fishing trawler. . . . And by the way," he said as an afterthought, "if any planes come out and have a look at us in the morning, I want you all below decks. All my crew have the right clothes to keep the make-believe going, and I don't want any plane to become suspicious at the numbers we are carrying aboard." He bade us a cheery good night and we turned in to some spare bunks. We were soon sleeping the sleep of the just and thankful.

Morning came with a bright blue sky, and I was on deck to see what sort of ship she was. Outwardly she looked a dirty, brown trawler, with bits of rope strewn everywhere and nothing at all shipshape. Some of the crew were working in old reefers, and the Captain was on the bridge in a garb not much better. It was on a closer inspection that the little trawler became interesting. The big steam winch was a 3.7 inch gun. Another gun was fixed aft under the guise of an engine-room hatch and machine-guns galore all over the ship could be swung into place in a jiffy. It must have been something like World War I's Q ships and looked quite effective.

We were going to be taken to Gibraltar, but first we had a mid-ocean rendezvous with a tiny coastal ship from which we would take about eighty Poles. This was quite a regular occurrence and many hundreds of Poles came out of Europe by this method. Our trawler never went in close to shore, but this was done by a little coastal ship about a quarter of our size and captained by a very gallant Polish sea captain. His guise was so good that he sailed right into small ports on the southern French coast to take aboard a new load to ferry out to our trawler. It was almost like a bus service, and was never suspected because of the tiny size of his craft.

We were at sea two days in a really bad storm, which made our little trawler stand on its head and tail alternately, with great seas sweeping over us from stem to stern. At times the bridge was the only part of us above the waves, and for the first time in my life I was seasick. So, too, were most of the crew for it was one of the worst summer storms that they had experienced in the Mediterranean.

We made our rendezvous with the Pole, but he was even worse off than we were and, in addition, had eighty wretched Polish refugees aboard packed like sardines in the open boat, under a tarpaulin that served to keep out most of the weight if not the wetness of the sea. After about twenty-four hours' cruising slowly around, the storm died down as quickly as it had blown up, and the eighty weary Poles climbed aboard us. The poor devils had not eaten or slept since they had embarked four days before, and their few possessions were soaking wet.

We dried them off and, with a good meal inside, their spirits perked up and they began to look more like human beings and less like half-starved animals. The little boat pushed off with its Polish captain, and we set course for Gibraltar at last. All the time we had been waiting for the weather to quieten we had been cruising between the Spanish-French frontier and Sardinia. We were never much more than fifty miles from shore and it was an anxious time lest a plane or ship should come out to see what we were doing. We were getting so close to home that it would be terrible if we were discovered now.

Everybody felt a bit easier when we had our load of Poles aboard, and even the crew could be seen going about their tasks a little more cheerfully than before. It must have been a thankless and a dangerous job that they were carrying out, and they received no recognition for it in the newspapers. All they could tell their friends and relations was that they were serving in H.M. Trawler ——, and that was all. They had the dangers and nerve strain of the submarine service without any of its glamour.

With thirty-six hours' sailing yet to do before we arrived at Gibraltar, our Captain announced that to-night would be "painting night." It was the thirteenth complete coat of paint that he had given his little ship in four months, and by morning we had to be a nice grey H.M. Trawler in all its glory with White Ensign flying, guns oiled, decks scrubbed and ropes neatly coiled everywhere. Everybody was dished out a pot of grey paint and a brush, and all night we painted, till by 4 a.m. the transformation had been completed and our little ship had had its face lifted again.

I don't think even we who had lived on the ship for close on six days had realised that there were so many guns aboard her. They seemed to sprout from every corner, and we would have given any attacker something to think about if he had poked his nose too close.

All the following day we sailed on westwards in the lovely Mediterranean sunshine, and now we began to feel we were really getting somewhere. We were due in at Gibraltar that night but would have to wait till dawn next morning before we were allowed in through the boom.

The authorities in Gibraltar were most surprised to find a party of escapers mixed up with the Poles, because nobody had warned them that we were coming. Everybody was very helpful, however, and somehow we were squeezed into a troopship that was sailing for Britain the next morning.

We dropped anchor off Gourock in the Clyde after ten days of zig-zagging in convoy across the Atlantic. On this occasion I was singled out by the Movements officer who came aboard. He had been told to get me to London as quickly as possible. An hour later I was seated in a fast train going south and had been the first passenger to leave the ship. I eagerly looked forward to a few days of enjoyment and renewal of old friendships and memories.

As I dozed, a feeling of deep satisfaction spread over me, a feeling of successful achievement, which in my conceit I thought I had justified. The sight of some W.V.S. (Women's Voluntary Service) doling out tea on a platform brought me to my senses. They were doing things for others. I realised then what I owed to all my friends still in prison in

Italy and to the dozens of brave Frenchmen and their wonderful organisation. If it had not been for them I would still be languishing behind barbed wire, with all the mental anguish and petty horrors which become magnified and distorted in so unnatural a life.

As I fell asleep I thanked God for my good fortune and prayed that others besides myself would have some of my luck.

Chapter XIV

TARANTO TO TERMOLI

AFTER TEN days' leave, I was on my way to Bulford to serve as Signal officer to Brigadier E. E. Down, who commanded the newly formed 2nd Parachute Brigade. It was wonderful to be able to do a useful job of work again and for the next six months we trained hard for the battles ahead.

In March 1943, we sailed for North Africa with the task of preparing for the invasion of Sicily. In this operation 2nd Parachute Brigade was ordered to capture Augusta by airborne attack, but the assault forces advanced so quickly in the early stages that the drop was cancelled. Our morale was very low as we went back to our hot and dusty camp in the olive groves near Sousse.

Two days later, on July 13th, we enviously watched the aircraft and gliders streaming overhead carrying 1st Parachute Brigade to their jump into Sicily, when they successfully captured Primasole bridge in spite of very inaccurate dropping on the part of the American aircrews. There was even a story told about one pilot who reported on return to base that he had carried out an accurate drop in spite of ack-ack fire. Actually he had flown south-west instead of north-east, and had given the signal to jump when over the Sahara, believing it to be Sicily.

The American sea assault into Sicily was also preceded by a very widely scattered drop on the part of 505th Parachute Combat Team, from 82nd Airborne Division. As in the case of the British operation, the troop carrier pilots had been blown off course by a strong cross wind which, when combined with ground haze, almost non-existent navigational aids and combat inexperience, resulted in only one man in eight being dropped within a mile or two of the right place. Neither the British nor the American airborne troops were dismayed by this apparent failure, and in many cases mere handfuls of men captured and held all their battalion objectives for the requisite length of time, until relieved by the ground forces from the beaches. The remainder, with a type of initiative and bravery that only airborne troops seem to possess, fought individual battles near to where they had been dropped and effectively prevented the move of German mobile reserves to the beachheads. One German general even said, after the war, that the entire success of the Allied Sicilian invasion was due to the way in which Allied airborne troops had blocked the movement of the German reserves.

The American commanders were deeply ashamed of the performance of their pilots. With characteristic thoroughness they instituted a period of intensive navigational training. By D-day the following year nothing but praise could be heard for the pilots who flew their unarmed and slow transport aircraft at a mere thousand feet to a pinpoint dropping zone over enemy territory.

On September 6th the whole 1st Airborne Division was given forty-eight hours' notice to embark at Bizerta for southern Italy. We were to be taken as deck cargo on five cruisers and a minelayer of the Royal Navy and one cruiser of the U.S. Navy.

By the evening of September 8th we sailed from Bizerta, with a bare minimum of transport. Jeeps and trailers were slung in odd places all over the ships and were even lashed to the tops of the gun-turrets. Next morning we heard of Italy's unconditional surrender and also saw the majority of Italy's battle fleet sailing past us going to Malta to give themselves up. That evening we disembarked at Taranto and by midnight had taken over intact the whole port and its important naval installations.

For the next three weeks 1st Airborne Division were the only allied troops in the "heel" of Italy. Taranto had to be held at all costs, and with the limited number of troops at our disposal all that could be attempted were a series of aggressive patrol actions on as wide a front as possible. These were singularly successful and 1st Airlanding Brigade were not withdrawn until they had reached Foggia, 120 miles from Taranto. By this time, 78th Infantry Division had landed, and had taken over from 1st Airborne Division who were brought back into reserve.

At the beginning of October our thoughts returned to the prisoners of war. What had happened to the thirty thousand British when Italy had capitulated? Apparently the War Office, acting on the advice of Allied H.Q. in Algiers, had told all camps that prisoners should remain where they were, and not try and come south to the Allied armies. This incredible blunder was based on the supposition that, if Italy capitulated, the Germans would withdraw to Austria, and would not oppose the Allied advance. The idea was that it was administratively much more convenient to deal with whole camps rather than have thirty thousand officers and men wandering about all over Italy.

Unfortunately, many camps obeyed these orders to the letter. At Chieti, for example, the Senior British Officer posted officer guards to prevent the remainder getting out. Only a few managed to escape the vigilance of their brother officers. The Germans arrived after a few days and removed the whole camp to Germany.

Similar scenes were enacted at many other camps. There is no doubt that this administrative mistake sentenced a great number of the officers and men who were prisoners in Italy at that time to an additional eighteen months of hell which they might have had a good chance of avoiding. Most of the facts leaked out into the press at the time but did not achieve the publicity they deserved.

Intelligence reports were coming through that, in spite of War Office orders, large numbers of officers and other ranks were wandering about Italy. The Germans had not bothered to take over the other ranks' camps straightaway, and in many cases the prisoners had become tired of waiting and had taken to the road. A few of the officer prison camps were occupied immediately by the Germans, such as the notorious Number 5 where Tag was, and the inmates were given no chances to escape. A few more officer camps had completely disregarded the orders and all were on their way, either going north to Switzerland or south towards our own lines.

The authorities now felt they should help the ex-prisoners get back by sea. The problem was how to contact them. Eventually it was decided to send in a number of small parties whose job it was to round up the maximum numbers and bring them down to a particular beach on the coast where they would be picked up by boat.

By the beginning of October several "round-up teams" had been landed along the east coast from Ortona to Rimini and one had been dropped by parachute a few miles inland from Pescara. An H.Q. to control the operations, together with the craft to be used for retrieving the prisoners, was established at Termoli.

No communications of any sort had been arranged to the round-up parties and it was soon realised that this was an extremely big handicap. A team had no way of telling the H.Q. in Termoli how many prisoners they had succeeded in collecting, or if they expected to be delayed, or even if the chosen beach was suitable. There was also no way of advising the team in the field of last-minute alterations, or breakdowns, or of passing on the latest intelligence information. Communications were obviously essential for success and 1st Airborne Division was asked to help.

I was then sent for by the General and told to see what could be done to improve the situation. "One last point, Tony," said General Down with a smile. "I want you to understand absolutely clearly that you will not set foot behind the German lines."

Two days later I arrived at Termoli together with some of my best wireless operators and a complete base wireless station. I planned to attach two wireless operators and their sets to any future collecting teams that were sent in by sea. We had been given for this purpose some midget wireless sets which were normally only issued to agents.

Termoli was a small natural port which had been improved with an artificial breakwater. The village was built

all round the harbour on the side of a hill and houses tum-
bled over each other in typical ramshackle style. Narrow
little alleys and streets burrowed their way between the
few tiny ill-lit shops and hovels in which the fishermen
lived.

The H.Q. had a house on the sea front, and when I went
to report to the Colonel I was shown into his office by a
swarthy-looking ruffian who mumbled in a strange language and wore a mixture of American and British uniform.
The Colonel was sitting at a rough wooden table covered
with Italian maps, and a cigarette hanging out of the corner
of his mouth. A bandage went right round his head and
under his chin, leaving a small shock of sandy hair sticking
out at the top. He told me later on that he was suffering
from some skin disease.

"Oh, I was expecting you," he said. "You have joined an
unconventional army here. The gangster who showed you
in is a Jugoslav agent and we have another as our officers'
mess cook. Our fleet consists of two Italian E boats complete with Italian naval crews, an L.C.I. manned by the
R.N.V.R. [Royal Navy Volunteer Reserve], and four Italian
fishing-boats equipped with ancient diesel engines. What
have you brought with you?"

I told him, and said that we could operate as soon as we
had set up our base station and had learnt how to use our
suitcase wireless sets.

Nearly every night during the next month I went up the
coast in one or other of our strange assortment of craft. On
one occasion we took the L.C.I. up to a beach fifty miles
north of Termoli expecting to take off three hundred prisoners. When we arrived only twenty-three were there, and

it turned out that not twenty minutes before we arrived over 250 had panicked when a burst of German schmeisser fire had been heard. One of the ex-prisoners of war had shouted, "It is a trap," and, in spite of the efforts of the officer in charge of the team, nearly all had streamed back to the farms and hills from which they had been collected.

On one night we had trouble with the Italian E boat commander. We were twenty minutes early and standing off the beach with engines stopped when a convoy of lorries could be seen moving south along the main road, which was quite close to the seashore at that point. He gave the order to start up the engines and return to port. I told him in my best Italian that unless he cancelled his orders he would die, and pulled out my Colt 45 automatic. He quickly changed his mind. Exactly on time I sent my sergeant off in an inflatable rubber dinghy to pick up six prisoners. I stayed on board to make sure that the Italian Navy did not go into reverse whilst the dinghy was paddling backwards and forwards, as it could only take two passengers at a time.

After a week or so, Naval Intelligence informed us that a minefield had been laid in a big rectangle along the coast to the north of Pescara. The Colonel decided to keep this a closely guarded secret from our Italian crews.

"If they hear that one," he said, "they will either be off like lamplighters or they will scuttle themselves in harbour here. That will only leave us the L.C.I. which is much too slow and usually too big."

The next night we took one of the fishing-boats up north through the supposed minefield to a midnight rendezvous on the coast. The old diesel engine sent up showers of sparks into the sky from its exhaust, and I felt sure we should be discovered when we went in close. This time, however, we received no recognition light signals from the beach and so we had to return empty handed.

One night when I did not go out, an E boat failed to return. We heard later that it had been engaged by a Light A.A. gun on the shore, and one of the torpedoes on the boat had exploded, blowing everything to pieces. Two of the British who had gone out that night were in the dinghy when it happened, and they had a sticky time avoiding capture for the next few days. They managed to return through our lines to tell their tale a fortnight after they had set out.

One day an Italian agent came in with a message from one of the parties that had been dropped over a month previously. A wireless set and operators were desperately required to pass back information about prisoners coming back through the lines. I was asked by Tony Simonds to provide them, and I called for two volunteers from my men. They naturally all wanted to go, but in the end I selected Sergeant P. Philips and Signalman D. Stewart, both Royal Signals. They were small in height and Sergeant Philips could have passed for an Italian anywhere, besides being a very expert and experienced wireless operator. Signalman Stewart was not quite so typical, having fair hair, but he had worked with Sergeant Philips for a long time and they knew each other well.

Two nights later I rowed the two ashore just north of Pescara, and wished them good luck. One was carrying the wireless set and the other a heavy accumulator when they climbed up the beach to start a series of adventures.

During the next week they tried to find the party which

had asked for them, but without success. In the end they gave up trying and decided to establish an escape team of their own. First of all they had to organise a regular flow of prisoners, then to discover a route through the German defences which was not being guarded, and then to collect parties of prisoners and lead them through to our own lines.

In addition, almost daily, Sergeant Philips came up on the air and sent through a brief message saying what was happening and what he proposed to do. When asked on one occasion how he was keeping his batteries charged for his wireless, he replied that he had set up his wireless in an attic over a German Brigade H.Q. At night he was charging his own batteries on a German engine that was running all night without supervision.

Almost every night for over a month Sergeant Philips and Signalman Stewart personally conducted a party of twenty to thirty ex-prisoners through the lines and went back for more. The Germans had wind of their activities and on three occasions they had to change their H.Q. and route. They only managed to clear out of one village by vaulting over some walls at the back of a farmhouse, and the wireless set had to be dumped in a pigsty. The Germans blew up the whole of that small village and shot all the men who were left.

Routes through the lines became more and more difficult to find till at last they decided to return themselves. They had brought through over four hundred prisoners, and were by far the most successful of all the teams. This was all the more remarkable as the Canadians were having a full-scale battle to capture Ortona over the same ground that Sergeant Philips brought back whole platoons of ex-prisoners every night.

Well did they deserve the personal congratulation by General Sir Oliver Leese who commanded the Eighth Army at the time, and the Distinguished Conduct Medals which were awarded three months later.

At the beginning of December we received word that the Division was returning home before Christmas, and I was ordered to hand over all our activities at Termoli to other troops.

First Airborne Division was to take part in the cross-Channel invasion after all, and we were all glad to be returning for what was obviously going to be the climax of the war.

Chapter XV

ARNHEM, SEPTEMBER 1944

I WOKE up cramped, thirsty and hungry. Was it yesterday that I had escaped from Italy, only to find myself to-day hiding in a tiny wall cupboard in Holland? My memory took me back the two years with a sudden vividness, and once more the horrors of life in a prison camp were hanging over me unless I could find a way out.

When 1st Airborne Division had returned to England nine months before, it had been given Lincolnshire as a base area, and nearly every village and town had its quota of troops wearing red berets. Large country houses, barns and stables were all requisitioned to house us and soon the whole country was strewn with unit direction signs, all bearing the Pegasus symbol of Airborne Forces.

At first the good Lincolnshire people were a little apprehensive. Were these troops a lot of undisciplined roughnecks, who would make their lives intolerable? Would it be safe to walk through the streets at night?

Their doubts were soon laid at rest when they saw a standard of discipline and smartness that they had never seen before in that part of the country. The villagers' feelings turned into admiration, and after only a few weeks they took a possessive pride in their local airborne unit. Arnhem Sunday is still celebrated throughout Lincolnshire

by parades of Old Comrades who return on an annual pil-
grimage from all over the United Kingdom.

We had to be ready for operations by the end of April,
barely four months hence. There was no time to lose and
we entered on a period of extremely intensive training, cul-
minating in divisional exercises in Yorkshire and in the
Cotswolds. By the beginning of May every man was convinced that he belonged to the best unit and the best Division in the British Army. This was reflected in their efficiency and enthusiasm both on exercises in the field and
in their country-house barracks in Lincolnshire. Our new
commander, Major-General R. E. Urquhart, was well liked
by all ranks, although he had not commanded airborne
troops before. A large man with an imposing figure, he was
too heavy to parachute, but everywhere he went he radi-
ated self-confidence. He himself planned to land by glider
with about half his H.Q. The other half would go to war by
parachute.

The Division consisted of two Parachute Brigades, one
Airlanding Brigade (gliders) and one attached Polish
Parachute Brigade. First Parachute Brigade consisted of
veterans from the North Africa and Sicily campaigns. It
was still commanded by Brigadier G. W. Lathbury, and
must have been one of the most efficient and battle-worthy
brigades in the British Army. Fourth Parachute Brigade
under Brigadier J. W. Hackett had been formed from British units in the Middle East and India, and although not so
experienced as 1st Parachute Brigade had an *esprit de
corps* all of its own. First Airlanding Brigade was made up
of ordinary infantry battalions who were carried to battle
in gliders, and was commanded by Brigadier P. N. W.

Hicks. The air-landing battalions were also very efficient and experienced and had been used in the initial glider assault into Sicily. In addition, there was the usual complement of gunners, sappers, signals and service troops. All these were on a much reduced scale when compared with a normal division, due to weight restrictions. I was second-in-command of the Divisional Signals and we had to make do with small wireless sets of much reduced power compared with those used in a normal division. We hoped that a higher standard of training would make up for some of the deficiencies of the equipment, and we were repeatedly assured that the Airborne Division would never be employed on a wide front, but would be landed and would fight within a small perimeter "perhaps as much as three miles in diameter."

D-day came on June 6th and with it the eternal question: "When is the Division going to be used, sir?" We read of great doings in France and felt sure we should be there too. We had worked the men up to a pitch of training that only action against the enemy would satisfy.

We soon had our answer. We had to prepare to land on the hills to the south of Caen in Normandy and help capture this important point in conjunction with 7th Armoured Division. We loaded up our transports and gliders, but on June 13th the operation was cancelled. Altogether seventeen operations were planned for 1st Airborne Division in the fourteen weeks between D-day and Arnhem, but of these only four came to the ears of the troops. Four times the aircraft were loaded up and four times unloaded again within a few hours.

After Caen it was Falaise, then south of Paris, and all

were cancelled. Tournai seemed a safe bet as it was on the road to Brussels and the British Army were getting very strung out in their rapid advance, but it, too, was quickly by-passed by the Guards Armoured Division and so became yet another plan not to be fulfilled.

The men's efficiency had reached a peak on D-day, but as each operation was put off, their spirits went down lower and lower. There was nothing wrong with them that action could not cure, but our standard excuses were wearing a bit thin after the fourth time.

"The main value of an airborne division," said a visiting brigadier, "is as a strategic threat to the enemy's lines of communications, which is lost as soon as the Division is landed." Arguments of this nature did not appeal to the men, however true they might have been, and officers had a difficult time keeping up their own as well as their troops' enthusiasm.

On September 12th yet another airborne operation was planned, this time to take place in Holland between Eindhoven and Arnhem. Two American and one British Airborne Divisions were going to be used and an Airborne Corps H.Q. Once again we loaded our aircraft and gliders; a task which had by now become a very well known drill and did not take long. The same old procedure of briefing the men took place and all the time we expected a cancellation to come through.

It was not till September 16th that I heard details of the whole operation. In general the task was to seize a fifty-mile-long corridor spanning eight major water obstacles including the Meuse, the Waal and the Lower Rhine at Arnhem. If this could be done, Field-Marshal Montgomery would be able to sweep forward into Holland and thence towards the vital Ruhr, thus turning the flank of the Siegfried Line, which ended at Aachen.

The planning had been done by 1st British Airborne Corps H.Q. under command of Lt.-General F. A. M. Browning, and there were many difficulties to be overcome.

In the first place, and by far the most important, there were only sufficient aircraft to lift about half the force. It was decided to allocate about a third to each Division, and this would mean that the landing would be spread over at least two days. Another solution which might have worked better was to give all aircraft, including fighter protection, to each Division in turn. Although some surprise might be lost, it would ensure that the Airborne Divisions, already pared to the bone to save weight, would have all their meagre resources available when asked to fight.

Lessons from previous airborne operations had all suggested that formations should be landed complete and as near to the objective as possible. Operation Market Garden split everything into two parts and was a risk only justified in face of negligible enemy opposition, and if the advancing ground forces could cover the fifty miles from Eindhoven to Arnhem in under two days. Both these suppositions proved to be wrong and it took Lt.-General B. G. Horrocks and XXX Corps seven days to reach the Lower Rhine.

The task given to 101st U.S. Airborne Division, under command Major General Maxwell D. Taylor, was to seize at least four big bridges over the rivers and canals which had to be crossed during the first fifteen miles of the advance. The next three bridges, including a big one over the

Waal at Nijmegen, were allotted to 82nd U.S. Airborne Division, under Major General James M. Gavin.

The task given to 1st Airborne Division was to seize the bridge over the Lower Rhine at Arnhem. Corps H.Q. had sent air photographs of the area and had suggested some dropping zones which were eight miles to the west of Arnhem on some open heathland.

The Corps air photographic experts said that Arnhem was heavily defended by flak, and that to fly closer than five miles to the town would invite up to two-thirds casualties in the slow-flying transport aircraft and gliders. They also said that the open farm country just south of the bridge would be too soft for landing gliders. Both these recommendations proved to be wrong. There were very few active flak guns and the ground south of the bridge would have been eminently suitable as a landing zone for gliders.

However, the experts' advice was taken and orders issued to use the dropping and landing zones west of Wolfhezen. As a result there arose yet another difficulty. As the Division had only enough aircraft to arrive in two waves (or in three if the Polish Parachute Brigade was included), a portion of the first day's wave had to stay on the dropping zone area to protect it for use twenty-four hours later. This weakened the striking force still further and moreover spread the Division over a large area of enemy-held country. If the enemy were to attack before the whole Division could be landed and concentrated on the objective, there would be a grave danger of being defeated in detail. Again the plan relied on negligible enemy opposition in the Arnhem area and again was found to be wrong. Ninth and Tenth S.S. Panzer Divisions were refitting near Arnhem and this fact had been sent by radio to London on September 15th by the Dutch Resistance, but was not received in time to affect the plan.

Another result of spreading the Division over such a big area was the inadequacy of the wireless sets with which we were equipped. They were designed to communicate up to three miles and all our exercises and operations had been planned and had worked on this basis. At Arnhem the sets would have to work eight miles to the bridge and fifteen miles to Corps H.Q. at Nijmegen. My advice was that communications would be most unreliable, especially in view of the built-up nature of the ground north of the river, but again this risk was accepted. Unfortunately, my doubts were proved in practice and communications were not established satisfactorily until the Division was fighting within a small perimeter.

Risks were taken in the Arnhem operation with eyes open. The prize was great if success came our way. If the German opposition had been as negligible as had been expected the whole plan would have been completely successful. The commanders concerned would have been congratulated on their nerve and timing.

Sunday, September 17th, 1944, dawned fine, and to our great surprise we had not yet received any cancellation. A lorry duly arrived at our Lincolnshire country house with our parachutes. An hour later more lorries arrived and we climbed aboard to go to an airfield near Grantham. Everything seemed so unreal. We had never got as far as this on any of our previous abortive operations.

All down one side of the airfield were some fifty C.47s, or Dakotas, lined up in staggered rows. We drove to our allotted aircraft and rechecked the loading which had been done on the previous day. Everything was all right and our American crews came over and helped us. They were a grand lot and mutual respect for each other had grown up in the preceding months. We could not have been served better, and but for them there would not have been any large-scale airborne operations.

The word came to put on parachutes and get into the aircraft. A few minutes later we were roaring down the runway at thirty-second intervals, and then flying in a wide circle, low over the villages we knew so well, while the rest took off and joined the armada. Now we were in tight formation, all fifty of us, flying south-east over the sunlit fen country. Looking out of the pilots' window I saw that my aircraft was the leader of our V formation and that half a mile ahead were another fifty Dakotas, flying steadily on, all bunched together. Behind us was a similar lot making one hundred and fifty in all, carrying 1st Parachute Brigade complete, together with the parachuting part of the Divisional Signals, and the Reconnaissance Squadron. The next day the same aircraft would bring the 4th Parachute Brigade, and the day after that the Polish Parachute Brigade, if they were required.

The glider element was taking off simultaneously from eleven airfields in Wiltshire and Hampshire, carrying two-thirds of the 1st Airlanding Brigade and the remainder of Divisional H.Q. and the Reconnaissance Squadron, in three hundred gliders. The towing aircraft were all found from No. 38 and No. 46 Groups R.A.F., and would return for a second lift of another three hundred gliders on the following day.

The flight plan phased in all the aircraft into one continuous stream and from the ground must have looked an impressive sight. From the air we could see the streets of the villages we passed over thronged with people looking upwards and an occasional handkerchief waving a farewell. It was midday when we crossed the coast and flew out across the North Sea, which for once was like a millpond with scarcely a ripple to disturb its brown-looking water.

The men in my plane were nearly all asleep by now as is the custom of the British private soldier. He had no worries, he placed supreme confidence in his officers and he often lacked all imagination. Little did he care that he was taking part in the biggest airborne operation ever launched; all that mattered was that he did his own job to the best of his ability. Therein lay his strength as a fighting soldier in adversity, and as events were to prove he was not found wanting.

Thirty-five minutes after leaving the Suffolk coastline there was a bustling amongst the crew in the cockpit up forward, and I could see them strapping on steel helmets. The Dutch coast was in sight and a few minutes later we flew in low over the island of Schonwen just south of Rotterdam. A moment later I saw several fighters with United States markings come up level with us for a second or two and then turn off and fly away out of sight. It was a comforting thought to remember that at least 1,200 fighters were on patrol to protect us during our flight. The Luftwaffe missed a golden opportunity on that Sunday morning.

A little later on we crossed the Dutch coast proper, and were surprised to see some Horsa gliders already landed in the fields below us. We heard later that about ten per cent had broken their tow ropes and had come down short of the correct landing zone.

The Dutch farms looked peaceful enough from above and there was no sign of any enemy. As in England, civilians looked upwards at us and an occasional handkerchief could be seen waving. I heard afterwards from a Dutch patriot, who watched us from below, that it was the most thrilling spectacle of his whole life, and surpassed even the day of his final liberation by the Canadians some eight months later.

There were now only twenty minutes left to the time we were due to drop and so far we had not suffered a scratch. No enemy fighters had come near, nor had any flak guns seen fit to fire in our direction. It was almost too good to be true, and I was just congratulating myself when a noise, like a sledge hammer beating the outside of our fuselage, woke up everybody, including my batman, Lance-Corporal Turner, who was an inveterate sleeper when in aeroplanes. Through our open doorway we could see a light flak gun shooting straight at us. Little yellow tongues of flame spat in our direction and a few seconds later some more hammer blows could be heard. There appeared to be no casualties so perhaps the shells were just grazing the fuselage, and this seemed to be confirmed when I saw about a foot of a wingtip suddenly disappear from the aircraft flying just opposite the open doorway, and only twenty or thirty feet away. We had just time to see six fighters diving down on the flak gun, all cannons blazing, and the German crew running for their slit trenches.

Still we droned on, and, after a signal from the pilot, I

gave the order, "Stand up, hook up and check equipment."
The whole plane load leapt into activity. Parachutes were
adjusted, static lines hooked on to the wire running down
the side of the fuselage, and steel helmets given a further
tighten up. Some looked a bit pale, others quite uncon-
cerned as I passed down the fuselage checking that each
man was properly hooked up. For many it was their first
operational jump, and after the incident with the flak gun
they were all most anxious to get the jump over and be on
the ground again. After hooking myself up, I took up position at the open door with the rest of the men as close as
they could get behind me. I could hear the engines change
their note as the pilot throttled down to jumping speed,
and, as a large river flashed by underneath, the red light
came on. That must be the Rhine and we were nearly there.
I could see some parachutes lying at the end of a field. An
enormous T had been laid out on the ground by the path-
finder company. "Green Light." I was out of the aircraft
and a moment later was gently swinging beneath my parachute.

All round me were parachutists as all fifty aircraft ejected
their loads. For those privileged to be there, it was a most
inspiring sight and one which I shall never forget.

I touched down in some heather and rolled over backwards, banging my head on a steel container in the process.
For a few seconds I could not think what I was doing, but
by now the next group of fifty aircraft was roaring overhead, and as if by magic another thousand parachutes came
out of their bodies and floated earthwards on top of us.

I had soon gathered my plane load and we were off towards the pre-arranged collecting point for Divisional

H.Q. An occasional rifle shot could be heard, but apart from this the whole landing operation could have taken place in England. There was hardly any wind and the sun streamed down on us. We had come down on a large open heath covered with heather and ringed by pine forests which gave out a singularly attractive scent, which contrasted with the tang of aviation petrol that hangs around military transport aircraft.

We arrived at the side of the heath in amongst a great clutter of crashed gliders. In one corner we met up with the rest of my men who had come by glider and, a little farther on, I could see the General and Lt.-Colonel C. Mackenzie, the General Staff Officer I of the Division. I reported all present and we were soon at work setting up the nucleus of a Divisional H.Q., based on the two or three jeeps that had already arrived, after being extracted from the tails of the gliders. Communications were established to 1st Parachute Brigade who were ready to move off within an hour of landing. It had been planned to send off the Recce Squadron under Major C. H. F. Gough to seize the Arnhem bridge by *coup de main*. The squadron was equipped with heavily-armed jeeps specially mounted with machine-guns pointing forwards and backwards. Unfortunately most of the gliders carrying his jeeps had failed to arrive due to broken tow ropes, and that part of the plan was discarded. For the time being, Divisional H.Q. would remain where it was, and we saw 1st Parachute Brigade moving off by companies through the trees towards Arnhem.

The two battalions of the 1st Airlanding Brigade to come in by glider, the 7th Battalion King's Own Scottish Borderers and 1st Battalion the Border Regiment, took up their defensive positions round the perimeter of the dropping zone. So far everything had gone to plan except for the Recce Squadron's jeeps.

Reports began to come in that 1st Parachute Brigade was meeting with considerable opposition on its way to the bridge. Three roughly parallel roads were being used for the advance, one for each battalion, and the southern one alone was found to be moderately clear of the enemy. Along this route Lt.-Colonel J. D. Frost and 2nd Parachute Battalion pushed as fast as they could, and by 8 p.m. that evening had established Battalion H.Q. and one company at the north end of the bridge. A little later a second company arrived and a large part of Brigade H.Q., the Signals section and some sappers.

In the meantime, the other two battalions in the Brigade had become heavily engaged in the woods when about half-way between the dropping zone and Arnhem. Brigadier Lathbury was visiting 3rd Parachute Battalion when it came under heavy fire, and a minute or two later General Urquhart arrived to join the Brigadier in a cellar which was being used for Battalion H.Q. Here both were forced to remain till early the next morning, but orders were issued to attempt to disengage the two northern battalions and push through to the bridge on the route used by 2nd Parachute Battalion.

The Division was now in three bits. Brigade H.Q., minus the Brigadier, together with most of one battalion were on the bridge, while the remainder of the Brigade were about two miles away on the edge of the town. The rest of the Division including Divisional H.Q. was back near the dropping zone. This was a military nightmare, which would

lead to disaster if the Germans attacked in strength. Luckily they attacked piecemeal, although precious little was
to be saved out of the mess.

Back at Divisional H.Q. on the first afternoon I was worried. Our communications back to the base in England
were weak and erratic, and being constantly interfered
with by a strong German station. We had no communication direct to Corps H.Q., although messages could be
sent via England. We had lost touch with 1st Parachute
Brigade H.Q., when they were only about five miles away
from our H.Q., in spite of every effort on our part to improve the position of our Divisional H.Q. sets. My Colonel
asked me to go forward as early as possible next morning
and see what the trouble was. He also ordered a change in
frequency for our main Divisional Command wireless set.
This change would not be known to 1st Parachute Brigade
unless they were informed, and he asked me to do this and
clear up the trouble. We had no idea at the time where
they had reached, or what the enemy was doing.

At first light on the eighteenth there was still no im-
provement and I set off with my batman, Lance-Corporal
Turner, who was an excellent man to have around in a
tricky situation. In peacetime he had been a valet-chauffeur
and nothing worried him. His dry sense of humour was an
asset anywhere and I have never before or since had such
fine and faithful service from anybody. By keeping our eyes
open we were able to avoid trouble, and scouted round
many pockets of Germans who were keeping up an irregular sniping action on the Brigade's route of advance.

Eventually we arrived at H.Q. 1st Parachute Battalion,
commanded by Lt.-Colonel D. Dobie, which had just

reached the outskirts of Arnhem proper, next to the St. Elizabeth Hospital. The battalion was preparing to attack with the aim of reaching the bridge through two miles of enemy-held streets. Lt.-Colonel Dobie had received his orders by wireless from Brigade H.Q. on the bridge, where Lt.-Colonel Frost was now acting as Brigade Commander.

First Battalion was now under concentrated fire from mortars and snipers. It was clear that the enemy had quickly appreciated our real purpose and was resisting with a surprising energy. Little did we realise that Field-Marshal Model, who commanded the German Army Group B, had his tactical H.Q. at Oosterbeek, not a mile from where we were, and had witnessed the drop on the previous day. He had immediately ordered armoured reinforcements from 9th S.S. Panzer Division, who as the Dutch had reported on the 15th, were re-equipping with the latest Panther tanks just north of Arnhem.*

Nobody of course knew of this at the time, and preparations for the attack went through with confidence. I managed to speak on the wireless to the Brigade Major, Major Hibbert, at Brigade H.Q., and tell him of the change in frequency, but, as they were still out of touch with Divisional H.Q. and I wanted to see how their communications were functioning, I decided to attach myself to the battalion and go through to the bridge with them. Like everybody else I completely failed to appreciate the strength of the opposition we were up against.

From the start the going was tough. I found myself in the position of encouraging some of the slower men in the battalion, who were cluttering up Battalion H.Q. One of

* *The Struggle for Europe* by Chester Wilmot (Harper & Brothers).

the companies, which had the job of clearing the river banks along the Rhine, was running into difficulties and Lance-Corporal Turner and I went forward to see what the trouble was. The company commander, who had been leading his men with great dash and energy, had just been killed. To take over seemed to be the only thing to do.

Street-fighting is always a pretty bloody business, and this was no exception.

About four hundred yards farther along our side of the river, just level with the pontoon bridge, the bank was broken by a thirty-foot wide channel leading to a small harbour in the middle of the town. A group of houses stood just short of the channel and I gave orders to capture and hold them while the rest of the battalion caught up with us on our left.

While we advanced under cover of the river bank, we were under constant small-arms fire, and at one point the Germans were able to toss stick grenades in our midst. These did little damage, and they soon stopped when we threw back our Mills bombs. Eventually we arrived at the group of houses, but only about twenty men were left out of the whole company. A little reconnaissance soon showed that we had left the rest of the battalion far to the rear and our position was quite untenable for any length of time. A check-up on our ammunition revealed that we only had about a hundred rounds between us, which was very little. The time was about 4 p.m. and I gave orders to take up defensive positions in the area. We distributed ourselves between three houses which gave us a commanding all-round view. Our big difficulty was that we had no way of telling Battalion H.Q. where we were or how successful our attack had been. I reckoned that the enemy would attack our position the following dawn, and unless we were relieved by then we would be in a sorry plight.

We kept up a sniping action to keep the Germans from getting too close, but by nightfall nearly all our ammunition had gone. From what little I could see, the battalion was still fighting in the area of the St. Elizabeth Hospital over eight hundred yards farther back. I decided that it was a hopeless position, and that our best course would be to try and get back to Battalion H.Q. by night, even if we had to swim the Rhine to avoid the town, where most of the Germans seemed to be placed. To give the best chance to everybody, the remains of the company were split into three groups, Lance-Corporal Turner and three other men coming with me. It would have been impossible to get twenty men back through the lines without being discovered. A lieutenant and a sergeant, whose names I do not know to this day, commanded the two other parties, and we all agreed it was the only practical solution. I decided to move to a house near the water as a jumping-off point, and broke in through a ground-floor window. We were just looking out of the window on the other side of the house when I heard somebody, obviously a German, trying to get into the front door of the house. I thought it most unlikely that we had been seen, and so we all dived into the lavatory and locked the door on the inside.

Eventually he broke in through the door, and to our dismay a section of about ten German soldiers followed him in and on upstairs. From the sounds of tile removing and furniture shifting, the house was being converted into a strong point in the German defensive position.

We sat in turns on that lavatory seat for the following three nights and three days until September 21st. During this time we could hear the almost incessant firing at the bridge just up the river, and the sounds of more distant fighting from the rest of the Division about three miles away. By night the sky was red with flames from burning houses, and occasionally lit up by a brilliant white light from a star shell or Very pistol. We were in an extraordinary position; a German machine-gun post above us and two more dug into the pavement outside the ground-floor windows. We would need luck to avoid capture in the predicament.

In the meantime, as I was to discover later, the advance by XXX Corps had been delayed. 101st Airborne Division had a very successful drop and, after some tough skirmishing, seized all its objectives, but unfortunately not before one bridge had been blown up by the fleeing Germans. This was to inflict a vital twelve hours' delay on the Guards Armoured Division, which was spearheading the British advance.

Eighty-second Airborne Division had also been dropped accurately and by the evening of the first day had seized all its objectives, except for the big bridge at Nijmegen, for which there were not sufficient troops available, due to shortage of airlift. The Germans quickly realised its importance to the Allied plan and made energetic efforts to defend it against all attacks. It was not till the second day after the landings that British tanks were able to reach the bridge and provide much needed fire support for a brilliant river-crossing operation by 504th Parachute Infantry, which enabled the far end of the bridge to be captured from the well dug in German defenders. This attack so impressed General Dempsey, the British Army Commander, that he told General Gavin, "I am proud to meet the commander of the greatest Division in the world today."

Unfortunately all these actions spelt delay, and the main advance, already forty-eight hours behind predicted timings, took another three days to reach the Rhine west of Arnhem.

At just about the same moment, I had decided, in my hiding place in the middle of the town, that I could stand it no longer and that we must make an attempt to get back that night—our fourth in hiding.

Often during those three days, Germans would come and try the door, but on finding it engaged politely went away and tried elsewhere. By the fourth night firing had died down considerably and apparently most of the Germans in the area had pulled out, although the post in our roof could be heard letting off a burst or two occasionally. My plan was to swim the river and, because of the current and our different swimming powers, we would rendezvous together on the far side at the blown railway bridge about a mile downstream.

We all took off our boots and heavier clothing and tied them inside our semi-waterproof smocks which could then be floated across the river without impeding our swimming. Our plan was to open the front door as quietly as possible and, using the shadows, walk down to the river not twenty yards away. The light from burning buildings in the bridge area was still annoying, but not half as bad as it had been on previous nights. I remember one of the men I had with me had quite a bad attack of jitters. He kept on saying, "We shall be cut to ribbons, sir, when we poke our noses out of that door." Actually he ceased to be frightened as soon as we started off, and I suppose his imagination had run riot while we had been cooped up in the lavatory all that time. He was a veteran of the North African campaign and had received the Military Medal while serving with the 2nd Parachute Battalion. We were all very hungry. I had eaten one concentrated ration on the evening of the seventeenth, but none of us had had anything since except some apples we found in the cellar of the house in which we were hiding. We would creep down in the middle of the night and lay in supplies for the day.

About 1 a.m. on September 22nd we crept out of the lavatory and opened the front door an inch or two. The machine-gun posts outside were no longer manned, although the equipment was still in position. The Germans must have been asleep nearby. Waiting for another phase of continuous firing, which I hoped would blanket the noise we would make, we quickly dodged from shadow to shadow and down to the river bank. A second later we were all swimming reasonably noiselessly. Occasionally a burst of firing would break out, and the reflections of burning buildings in the water made me feel that we could not help being seen. As we came out into the current, I was rapidly swept downstream and lost touch with the rest of the men. The Rhine at this point was about four hundred yards across and due to the distance I swam as slowly as possible to avoid getting overtired or out of breath. Eventually the chimneys of a brick factory loomed above me and I was clambering up the slippery bank. I had hoped that the Second Army might have reached that bank by now for if they had not done so they would be three days behind schedule. However, I was not going to take any risks, and would move as though the enemy were in possession.

Having untied my bundle and put on my clothes, which were surprisingly dry, I started to move slowly down the river bank to the railway bridge, where I had planned to meet the rest of the men. It would have been better to have chosen a closer rendezvous, but this was the only unmistakable one, and seemed the easiest for them to find. The time was now 2:30 a.m. and we only had three hours left before dawn. Slowly I walked or crawled along the bank, straining my eyes and ears for any sounds of the enemy. A burning haystack on one side showed that the area was still active and now and again I could hear firing coming from my front. After about an hour and a half I began to see the outlines of the old railway bridge about four hundred yards away which was occasionally brilliantly lit up by a star shell. During all this time I saw nothing of the men, which was surprising because we all should have been moving down the same way.

I was getting quite close to the bridge when I had to leave the river bank to skirt round a dyke which flowed into the Rhine. I was just getting over a wide ditch when I heard a shrill whistle blown about thirty yards away. It was still about one hour before dawn. I suddenly realised what had happened. The Germans were manning the railway embankment leading to the bridge and were "standing to" an hour before dawn, as is the custom in the British Army. This is to ensure that all defences are manned in case of a dawn attack and is almost standard front-line procedure in any army.

What accursed luck I had! I was now in the German front line with only a few yards to go, and I had arrived in time for the German "stand to." I quickly ran forward; with any luck I might still beat them to it and was just climbing up the embankment when I fell into a slit trench on top of a German who was bending down at that moment. He started shouting and one of his pals came over from his trench, about two yards away, to find me struggling with a rather sleepy German in a wet trench some four feet long and about four feet deep.

Chapter XVI

CUPBOARD LOVE

THE GAME was up and I was a prisoner again. Once more I went through the indignity of being searched by the enemy, but on this occasion I at least had no weapons to surrender. I had had to let go my sten gun and pistol whilst swimming across the Rhine.

No longer was I a free man and the anti-climax suddenly made me remember my hunger, and how every bone and muscle in my body ached for rest. Wearily, so wearily, I was marched down the road to the Company H.Q., watched by sleepy-eyed Germans from slit trenches dug into the verge.

We stopped at a farmhouse and I was shown into a room, after pushing aside a blackout blanket which had been nailed over the doorway. Inside, a hot aroma of unwashed bodies, the acrid stench of stale German tobacco smoke and seasoned sausage, combined to stifle my nostrils. A hurricane lamp turned low gave the only light, and in the gloom my smarting eyes could now see gently-heaving bodies wrapped up in greatcoats lying all over the floor, with mounds of equipment taking up every vacant space. The only sounds were wheezes and snores, except for the faint noise of a conversation in German coming from a next-door room.

One of my escort of three pushed by and, after mumbling what I took to be swear words, woke up one of the prostrate Germans. He turned out to be an N.C.O. and was soon kicking the other bodies to life, who grunted in a dialect I did not understand, and then stood up and stretched. A piece of paper passed hands and I was off again out of the house with three new guards to Battalion H.Q. which was about a mile away.

This time everything was much more orderly, and after a German sentry had examined the piece of paper carried by my escort, we went down some steps into a cellar whose roof had been chocked up with large baulks of timber. A clean-shaven, middle-aged German subaltern sat at a table with a lamp on one corner. He motioned me to sit down and said in broken English:

"I must to you questions ask. You will answer."

"Oh."

"Your name, please?"

I told him.

"What day you jumped?"

"I can't say."

"How many more are you?"

"I can't say."

His eyes seemed to bulge a bit behind his glasses, and an angry flush spread up his neck.

"O.K. You no speak. We will see."

He ended with some instructions in German and I was shown outside into the back of an open volkswagen car, in which I was driven along the road towards Arnhem.

We crossed the Rhine using the main bridge for which so many lives had been sacrificed. I could see many marks of the bloody fighting which had taken place as we threaded our way in and out of shell holes and burnt-out German tanks. Smoke was still coming from the ruins of the buildings on the north side of the river.

We sped on through deserted streets to the outskirts of the town and stopped outside a newly-built church which had sentries posted all round it. I was told to get out and wait inside. There I found the church full of newly-captured prisoners of war standing in little groups everywhere. In one corner I could see a few officers, none of whom I knew, and I learnt from them that the Division was now fighting inside a small perimeter round Oosterbeek, a suburb located about three miles from the centre of Arnhem.

In another corner I saw Lance-Corporal Turner and the three others who had shared the lavatory with me. They too had been captured that morning in various places not far from where I had been taken. All touch had been lost while swimming across, and Turner had been caught whilst trying to find a hiding place in a farmhouse. Daylight had come before he had reached a point anywhere near the railway bridge.

We all looked pretty scruffy in that church. I had a five days' growth of beard, not having had a chance to shave, and many were like me. All had the slightly haggard and drawn look of soldiers who have been without sleep, and seen their best friends die, not knowing when their own turn might come. Some were rummaging in their pockets or haversacks for any crumbs left over from the once despised forty-eight hour concentrated ration that we all carried. Many were lying down full length on the pews fast asleep, snoring away with mouths slightly open and heads twisted at any angle.

As the morning drew on, the air in the church became warmer, and more and more of us lay down where we were on the hard tiles and went fast asleep. I followed suit after checking that all doors were guarded and there was no way of getting out.

The Germans still gave us nothing to eat and by midday we were all getting very hungry and thirsty. Some men I spoke to asked me if I could get the Germans to do something about it.

After some argument I managed to get hold of an officer who could speak some English and in a mixture of the two languages I told him that we expected to be given food within an hour, or else I would see that his name was remembered after the war when the time came to deal with the war criminals who disobeyed the Geneva Convention.

He became quite angry and spluttered:

"You can all think yourselves lucky to be alive and you will get food when it pleases us. Anyhow what do you know about Geneva Conventions?"

"You would be surprised," I replied; "but food we must have, and it is your responsibility to provide."

"Let me tell you, Herr Major, I have just received orders to march you all to a prison near here run by the S.S. I am sure they will feed you."

With a glint in his eye, he turned on his heel, and five minutes later we were on the march with guards on all sides. For two miles we went through the suburbs and saw very few civilians; one or two of them were brave enough to wave and smile as we went by.

Eventually we arrived at a house on the outskirts of Arnhem in another suburb called Velp. This was used as a prisoner of war cage and was guarded by an understrength company of fifty-five men. It was a typical large suburban house, about twenty yards back from the main road and with exactly similar ones on either side. Two monkey-puzzle trees stood on the front lawn.

Inside the house were about five hundred all ranks of the Division, whose spirits were high except for the ignominy of being prisoners. Here I met Freddie Gough, Tony Hibbert, and many others. I learnt all their news and told them mine. The Germans fed us on tins of lard and coarse brown bread, but we were not fussy and I wolfed my share down. I had not had a really square meal since leaving England, my last being breakfast on the seventeenth, and to-day was the twenty-second. What months it all seemed, and yet it was only five days.

I heard that the bridge had been captured by the Germans soon after dawn on the twenty-first, when nearly all the original defenders were killed or wounded, and all ammunition had been expended. Colonel Johnny Frost had himself been wounded, and for the last twenty-four hours Freddie Gough had been in command. For three days and nights this gallant force had held out against overwhelming odds, including tanks, which came up and gradually knocked down or set on fire every house that was being used for the defence. Some of these tanks had been stalked on foot and blown up with grenades. Fighting patrols had gone out every night to drive the Germans out of houses which overlooked the bridge. Deeds of heroism were done which are matchless in the history of the British Army, but received little publicity at the time because nobody returned to tell the tale. The Division had been ordered to hold the bridge for forty-eight hours until the arrival of the Second Army. It had been held for seventy-two hours by six hundred men, but unfortunately to no avail.

We now realised what a failure the whole operation had been, but we still hoped that the Division could hold on where it was and provide Second Army with a bridgehead through which the advance could continue. Many were our speculations on what was happening to the rest of our units still fighting, but our hearts were heavy and we could not help thinking about ourselves and our present plight.

I remember the latrines inside the house were hopelessly inadequate for the numbers of men, and some deep trenches had been dug at the bottom of the garden at the back of the house. In this garden were growing carrots and onions, and we quickly dug these up and distributed them on the basis of half a carrot or onion per head. It took some of the hunger away.

All this time I was looking for ways out of the house or garden. I was determined to escape and not be a prisoner longer than I could help. Now would be the time and it would be infinitely easier than later on.

Some of the officers were already saying that they would leave trying to escape till they arrived at the German prison camp. It would all be "laid on" there. It is so easy to put off action till to-morrow and all this sort of talk was so reminiscent of my experiences in Italy. I told everybody I saw that their one and only chance of getting away would be before they left Holland. The farther they went back along the evacuation channels, the more difficult would escape become. I think they believed me, but most of them could not see any possible way out with any hope of success. When I started looking over the whole house and the garden, there were many smiles cast in my direction. It was not possible to get away they said, they had already been over the place with a fine tooth comb. The trouble was that most of them were numbed by the anti-climax of being prisoners, and they did not realise that, small though the chances of getting away were at the moment, they would be better now than at any future date.

I reasoned that the cage would only be temporary and would last as long as the Division did. From all accounts this would not be long, so one solution would be to hide up in the house itself till the Germans left and then to get out. Again it was just possible that the Second Army would continue their advance through the Division's bridgehead, and then the area would be liberated.

I could not see any way to escape that gave a better than fifty-fifty chance of success, so I looked everywhere for a hiding place that would hold me for two or three days. The only possible place seemed to be a wall-cupboard in one of the ground-floor rooms, which had a flush-fitting concealed door. The whole door was covered with the same sort of wallpaper as that of the rest of the room, and was difficult to see except on close examination. The cupboard was about four feet across, twelve inches deep, and about seven feet high. Its interior was divided horizontally by adjustable shelves, but by removing the shelves I was able to stand inside in tolerable comfort. Fastening the door was a problem. The cupboard was fitted with the normal type of mortice lock let into the thickness of the door, with a keyhole on the outside complete with key. By unscrewing the lock, and turning it back to front, the keyhole came on the inside of the door and I was able to lock myself in. A piece of wallpaper, torn from another part of the room and pasted over the outside keyhole, helped to conceal the cupboard's presence.

The next job was to lay in a stock of water and food. All I had was my waterbottle, and I found an old two-pound jam jar that I also filled up. A one-pound tin of lard and half a small loaf of bread completed all the provisioning I could do. Some of the officers very kindly offered to give me their waterbottles, but I refused. They would need them for their own escape, which, I reminded them, they must try to make or be a prisoner for the rest of the war.

Little did I think that I would be confined to my cramped little cupboard for thirteen days and nights before getting out. I thought that the limit of my endurance would be reached after three or four days, because I did not start off in the best condition for an endurance test. The Germans came round on the evening of the twenty-second to take all names, and in order to avoid a record being taken I started standing in my cupboard. Pole squatting is, I believe, a time-honoured sport in the U.S.A. I cannot recommend cupboard standing to anybody who wants to try out something new. I stood first on one leg then on the other; then I leaned on one shoulder and then on the other. There was no room to sit down because the cupboard was too shallow. I managed to sleep all right, although occasionally my knees would give way and would drop forward against the door making a hammer-like noise. Every bone in my body ached, and I felt quite light-headed from lack of food, water and rest.

The day after I locked myself in the cupboard the Germans turned the room into an interrogation centre. Every officer and man going through that cage was first interrogated in the room where my cupboard was. It was certainly an interesting experience, which I believe has never before been rivalled, though I scarcely appreciated its uniqueness at the time. We in the army had always been instructed that if ever we were made prisoner, the only information that we should give was our army number, rank and name. The Germans knew this, of course, but tried every guile to get more information. The usual trick was to pretend that they were filling out a card for the Red Cross, and ask a series of innocuous questions until the prisoner was at ease, when a question of military importance would suddenly pop up. It was a surprising thing to me that very few officers or men gave only their number, rank and name. Almost everybody gave a little additional harmless information, such as the address of their parents or wives, or whether they were regular soldiers or had been in the Territorial Army before the war.

Only two gave away military information. One was a captain in the Glider Pilots, and another was the batman to a company commander of the leading battalion of relieving Second Army. This battalion had assaulted across the Rhine opposite the Division's perimeter in order to allow the successful withdrawal of the Division. These two men, who shall be nameless, gave all the information they knew or were capable of giving. Luckily neither was in possession of any real military secrets and no great harm was done, except to my pride. The officer talked so much, and seemed so promising a source of information, that he was given lunch just in front of my cupboard door. What agonies of mind and tummy! To hear all this coming out, and to smell what seemed to be a delicious meal only a few yards from my hiding place! I nearly burst out of the cupboard on several occasions to stop the wretch giving information. I think I would have done so if he had started to say anything serious. Luckily he did not know much and I kept my peace and exercised self-control over my mental anguish.

The questioning went on for several days, four or five I think, and by night the room was used as sleeping quarters for the German guard. I had no chances to get out at all, but as I had lasted so far, I resolved to try to remain a little longer. My luck must come to my rescue. It had always done so up till now.

Little by little I eked out my rations of water and bread. Four mouthfuls of water every four or five hours and just a bite or two of bread. The water was the chief shortage, and after nine or ten days I could not eat any more bread because my mouth was so dry. For the benefit of the curious, I was able to direct my urine through a paper funnel into one corner of the cupboard where there was a gap in the floor boards to allow some pipes to pass down to the cellar. It interested me to see that I continued to pass water in spite of drinking practically nothing. I did not feel the need to do anything more solid during the whole time, perhaps because there was nothing in my tummy. My system started to function again quite normally as soon as I started to eat when I got out. My only legacy was a series of bad boils, followed by styes, which persisted for about a year afterwards.

It was now October 5th, 1944, and the thirteenth day of my voluntary confinement. My water was nearly at an end, and the cramp in my muscles hurt acutely most of the time. Patience and caution were now finished and I told myself that I would have to make an attempt to escape that evening or fail in the effort.

The room outside my cupboard was still full of Germans but, provided no new prisoners came in that evening, there would be a good chance of the whole guard leaving the room empty for half an hour or so at sunset. On the previous evening they had all cleared out of the room and hung over the garden wall adjoining the main road outside my window, to watch the passers-by in the twilight. I suppose it is a world-wide habit to come out of the houses on a warm evening for a breather before going back inside for the night. The only thing that might spoil it would be new prisoners; but there had not been any last night, so with any luck I would get away to-night.

I slowly shifted my weight from one leg to the other, and leaned alternately on my right shoulder and then my left. By now, shifting my position had become almost automatic, and no longer required any thought or even consciousness. My mouth was dry as a bone, but I had already had both my dawn and midday mouthfuls. My evening one was not due for another two hours yet. To-night I would take three mouthfuls of water. What bliss this promised to be!

It was due to get dark about 7:30 p.m. or 8 p.m., and I hoped the room would clear by about 7 p.m. I would then have to hide up in the bushes near the house for an hour, till it was really dark before it would be possible to move round to the back of the house and get away.

The minutes slowly crept by while I waited anxiously, my ears taut for the sound of the Germans leaving the room. Occasionally one of them would go in or out, but I could hear snores from two or three having an after-lunch nap. At about six o'clock I pulled on my boots and smock and gathered all my equipment. Dressing in that cupboard was a work of art, and to avoid making a noise it was three-quarters of an hour before I was ready. While I was dressing I heard two Germans stumble out of the room, but I was fairly certain that there were one or two more. Sure enough, by their grunts and the bumping of boots on the floor, I heard two more get up and go out talking about a *fraülein*.

The time had come. Cautiously I unlocked my door. There might still be the odd squarehead making up arrears of sleep. I opened the door an inch and had a quick look round. Damnation take it, there, not six feet away, was a solitary German soldier sleeping with his hands crossed over his tummy and his mouth wide open. As I had to walk across the floor and open the big french windows, which were both noisy operations, I decided to give him another half hour.

A few troops came clattering into the building with a couple of girls, all talking at the tops of their voices. I heard them go upstairs and enter the room directly over my head, and they soon had quite a merry party going with songs and a gramophone, and an occasional girlish giggle or scream. I was in luck. They were probably not expecting any prisoners to-night, and if the noise increased as the wine flowed I should have no worries about covering up squeaks as I opened a window.

The noise upstairs woke up my sleeping soldier after about twenty minutes, and he got up and walked out. This was my chance and, taking a couple of mouthfuls of water, I gently pushed the door open again. This time the room was empty. I could see the guards lining the garden fence on the main road and not ten yards away. My plan was to get the window open and then wait for a lorry or tank to go by before slipping out and into the shrubs growing almost under the sill. Germans would be most unlikely to look back towards the house when anything interesting was passing.

I was in luck and no sooner had I opened the windows when a large truck went clattering by. This was my cue, and I was quickly out and had dropped into the shrubbery. My luck held good on the thirteenth day in that Dutch cupboard.

I quickly crawled into the bushes where they were thickest at the corner of the house, and concealed myself as best I could with dead leaves. From where I was, I could see eight or ten of the guard idly leaning against the garden fence a few yards away and could hear them chatting unconcernedly about the war in general and their sweethearts at home. From the window above came occasional strains of gramophone records and the semi-delighted, semi-frightened squeals from the not-too-particular girls.

Chapter XVII

DUTCH COURAGE

IT GRADUALLY grew dark and one by one the Germans left the fence and went back inside the house. Forty-five minutes later it was black enough to start moving, and stealthily I crept to the back and climbed over the fence into an adjoining garden. The bottom part of the garden was all vegetables and I quickly pulled some beetroots up, wiped off most of the mud on the seat of my trousers, and chewed them eagerly. The juicy sweetness of the beetroot tasted wonderful, but I don't suppose it did my stomach much good. From the garden I climbed through another fence into an orchard and was soon feasting on some excellent apples. I would not have bothered about the beetroot if I had known about the orchard, and rapidly I munched my way through half a dozen apples. I could feel renewed strength and vitality seeping back into my veins and I stretched my arms and legs with the joy of freedom and relief from that terrible cupboard. My legs were incredibly weak but I was now full of hope and my brain was again functioning more or less normally.

My plan was now to contact a friendly Dutch family, who might give me some civilian clothes. Once I had these, I should not find it too difficult to move about and find a way back to our own lines. I decided I might as well try the houses nearby. If the Germans did suspect that the cupboard had housed an escaper, which I thought most unlikely, then they would never guess that he was hiding within a few hundred yards of his late prison. Also the more I moved around with a sixteen-day beard on my chin, the more likely I was to be discovered.

Stuffing a few apples into my pockets, I moved down to the bottom of the orchard where it joined on to some gardens at the back of a row of houses. The fence was a high one and made of close-mesh wire, but I soon found a hole underneath and wormed my way through. The houses were the usual brick-built semi-detached suburban types, and I could see no reason against tapping on the door of the first one I came to, telling them who I was, and asking for shelter.

I tiptoed past a coal shed and knocked gently on a door of a house with its bottom windows still lit up but screened with black-out curtains. Eventually I heard a voice asking who was there in Dutch. In halting German I stammered out:

"I am a British parachutist. Please give me food and shelter."

"Go away quickly," he replied in equally bad German, "my house is full. We have no food. Very dangerous to have you here."

The whole conversation was conducted through the closed door and in the end he did not wait for me to answer and I heard him stamping off to another room.

Disconsolately I walked back a few paces and decided to rest in a small coal shed to collect my thoughts before my next move. I would cross the road and try a house on the opposite side. I would go round to the back where perhaps I might find a more friendly family than the one which I had tried first.

I came out of the shed and, after passing between two houses, crouched in the shadow of a wall while a German army truck full of troops swept by. As soon as it had rounded the bend, I walked quickly across the road and between two more houses on the opposite side. Once more I tapped on a door but to no avail. The time was now about 11 p.m. and all were in bed.

I tried three more houses and still got no reply. But I noticed saucers left lying outside the back doors of all three houses; they were full of scraps off plates and presumably left for cats. I was so hungry that I went from door to door wolfing the scraps which really tasted excellent. Eventually I had had quite a reasonable meal, and I decided that the best plan was to hide in one of the sheds at the back of the houses and wait there till morning. I chose the one which had the biggest plate of scraps—they surely must be charitable people—and soon nestled down in an old potting shed full of seed trays and broken furniture. I slept well and woke at dawn to watch for any sign of the inhabitants so that I could make myself known to them as early as possible. Gradually I heard the house wake up: the alarm clock go off, sleepy yawns come from a window, and finally a man looked out at the morning sky. Half an hour went by and the back door was opened so that I could look straight into the kitchen where a girl of about twenty was cooking on a stove and a man swept out the kitchen and then cleaned his shoes. Eventually he shaved, put on his jacket and came towards my hiding place, presumably to get some firewood.

As he came in through the door I said, "Good morning" in German, and, to give him his due, he did not appear to be in the least taken aback. Speaking German in whispers I told him my story and asked him if he could help. He understood me quite easily and replied that he would do his best but that there were a lot of children nearby who might stumble on me whilst playing and give me away. He said he could not hide me in his house, but he would try to find a place where I could go that night. He would also see about some food. I thanked him with a terrific handshake and with a wink he turned towards the house and beckoned his wife to come over to the shed.

At first she would not do so; but after a bit she came over, looking rather cross, and walked into the shed. She suddenly saw me and let out a scream, clutching her husband for protection and looking thoroughly frightened. I do not suppose I was a very edifying sight, with my ginger beard, camouflage airborne smock, and torn, dirty battledress trousers. It was the first time, and I hope the last, that a woman has screamed with terror on seeing me. However, her fears were soon put at rest and she went back to the house with her husband to prepare a meal, although still with a rather scared look in her eyes.

In the meantime I had a look round my hut to find a possible hiding place in case any children came near, or the Germans made a search. There were some horizontal wooden beams under the roof, and at one end a few planks had been placed across them to hold up some bales of straw. At first sight this looked the best hiding place, but its big disadvantage was that it was also easily the most obvious. Anybody coming into that hut would immediately be attracted by the pile of straw up in the roof. I therefore decided to hide under a pile of loosely-stacked seed boxes and apple trays that littered the floor. By arranging these in the manner of a tunnel I crawled in underneath and pulled some old sacks on top of me. Even if somebody had peered down through the clutter of trays, he would only have seen a pile of sacks at the bottom.

Hiding, always hiding! What a monotonous and horrible business! But I could not afford to walk about in daylight, unwashed, unshaven and dressed as I was. Before I had had time to make myself really comfortable the good lady of the house brought out an enormous plate of boiled potatoes over which she had poured a savoury gravy. It smelt like a banquet fit for kings. I had soon wolfed this down and then swallowed about a pint of ersatz coffee, which made me feel as if I had not slept for weeks.

I woke up to the clink and thud of heavy military boots tramping in the yard outside and the sound of German voices. From the snatches of conversation I gathered that they were accusing the Dutchman of sheltering a British officer. In halting German he flatly denied the accusations, but I could imagine him being brushed aside and I could hear the Germans walking upstairs and banging open doors and cupboards. I was scared stiff and pulled the sacks even closer, hoping against hope that they would leave out my shed. Obviously the news of my presence had leaked out and the German security police were already on my trail. What a horrible thought!

I then heard them come banging downstairs, out into the yard and straight towards my hut. I could hear someone's heavy breathing as he paused just inside the doorway to allow his eyes to get used to the gloom, and also the expostulations of my good Dutch host in the background. As I had thought, the first place he looked at was the straw up in the rafters. Muttering oaths, the German climbed up and pulled away at the straw bales which came crashing down to the floor. As soon as he had satisfied himself that there was nobody there, he did not bother to look anywhere else and left the shed, after which I could hear them leaving the courtyard to go somewhere else. Once again my luck was in, and I was round another tight corner.

About four o'clock the Dutchman came back, and with a voice shaking with agitation, told me I would have to leave straightaway. I replied that I would wait till dark, and in the meantime would he find somebody who would be prepared to take me in. The poor man was obviously in a complete dither and nearly incapable of any speech which was not really surprising. I asked him if he knew why the Germans had come, and he said he thought that it must have been the children who had given me away.

Evening came and he returned with an aluminium canteen full of sandwiches and a waterbottle full of milk. He was obviously longing for my departure but felt a bit guilty at turning me away, and so gave me all the food he could spare. When it was quite dark he led me outside and told me to follow the railway line for about a mile, when I should find open country on my left wing with a big white farm whose owners, he thought, would shelter me for a short time. Thanking him profusely for his kindness, I was soon on my way, walking down the cinder path alongside the railway track. It was pitch dark which was a help, and my host had told me that the line was free from German patrols.

I soon recognised the farmhouse and found the back door, upon which I gave an urgent Victory V tap. The door opened a crack and in a whisper I told the farmer who I was. He replied that German patrols were all round his house, and he could not help me, after which to my amazement he slammed the door in my face.

I walked away, and half a mile farther on I tried another house only to get the same treatment. By 10:30 p.m. I had walked two or three miles and tried two more houses with no success. I was very tired and disheartened and started wondering what on earth I should do if I were unable to find shelter by daybreak.

I heard a church clock chime eleven and decided to look for the vicarage and ask the parson to help me. The church was across some fields surrounded by trees, and after I had walked there I found a building joining on to it which would presumably be the vicarage. A light shone under the door, and I tapped gently for an entry which was only given me after five minutes' anxious waiting outside.

A young priest dressed in a long black cassock was standing holding a lantern in one hand, while a group of about a dozen men, women and children were crowding round behind him interested to see who was knocking so gently after curfew hours. I quickly told him my story, and he said that although he could not let me stay in the house he thought he would be able to help me. Apparently I was in a Roman Catholic school that had been partly requisitioned to house some German troops serving an A.A. gun in some

trees nearby. The remainder of the house was full of evacuees from Arnhem, and therefore it was a most unsuitable
choice as a hiding place. My luck was in again. If I had
tapped at the wrong door it would have been opened by a
German and not the parson.

I was the centre of attraction, surrounded by about a
dozen evacuees of all ages, with a couple of young priests
hovering in the background. A large cup of milk was
brought and was very welcome. Then followed a long dis-
cussion about where I should go, and eventually they decided to send for the school's private policeman who lived a
few hundred yards away.

At last, a real old character walked in. He looked more
like a gamekeeper than a policeman and was dressed in a
black corduroy jacket and breeches with black leather leg-
gings and boots. His hat was a green "pork-pie" and his face
was thin and lined, but he had a twinkle of amusement in
his eyes. Although he could not speak a word of English, he
was obviously enjoying himself immensely. This was his
chance to do something for Holland, and get fame as a
patriot. I imagine his life must have been rather dull until
now, and secretly he must have longed to take a more active
part in the war, although his family would no doubt have
kept him from doing anything rash.

He led me out through the school doorway and down an
avenue of trees to his cottage at the end of the road. The
time was about midnight, and his wife was waiting up for
his return. A genial, fat old soul, she produced some bread
and jam and I further sated my almost inexhaustible appetite. It must have been a strange scene. A shaded lamp stood
on a shelf on one side of the room, in the middle of which

was a heavy wooden table with a scrubbed top. Shining copper cooking pots hung over the stove while round the walls there were all sorts of bric-a-brac on shelves and brackets.

The old lady in nightgown and curling papers kept a perpetual fixed smile on her face, while her husband tried to tell me his life history in Dutch. I sat at the table munching the bread, at the same time feeling rather uncomfortable with my filthy hands and heavy growth of beard on my face. Naturally I had not washed or even taken off my clothes since leaving England, although I had managed to have a quick shave soon after I arrived in the prison cage at Velp.

After washing down the bread with some strange beverage which was called tea, and made from dried apple and blackberry leaves, the old man suggested that I should shave and take off all my uniform. He would get me some clothes in the morning and it would be safer if he hid all evidence of his "Tommy" as he called me. After shaving with his old cut-throat razor, we climbed upstairs to the attic, one end of which had been converted into a bedroom. I was soon fast asleep between cool white sheets—what fantastic luxury!

The sun was streaming into the room and outside my window I could see an apple tree laden down with enormous red apples. My watch told me it was twelve o'clock, so I had slept continuously for about twelve hours. I lay back luxuriously in my bed and wondered what would happen next. I did not feel inclined to do anything except take it easy and recover some of my lost strength. Until now I had not realised quite how weak I was. Nervous energy and excitement had been my fuel, but now natural processes had caught up and all I wanted to do was to lie back and breathe in the beautiful fresh free air and thank God that I was not a prisoner of war.

Suddenly the familiar whine of a shell passing overhead, followed by an explosion a field or two away, brought me to my senses. I remembered that war was only a few miles away, and thought that I had better do something about getting back across the lines. I climbed out of bed and literally tottered across to the window. A mirror over the washstand gave me a shock. A more cadaverous, thin, lined face I have yet to see, and I could hardly believe that I was looking at myself. Outside, beyond some beautiful green fields across which I had trudged the night before, lay Velp and the outskirts of Arnhem. The shell I had heard pass had landed in amongst some cows, and I could see a farmer hurrying out to see what damage had been done. Milk was so short, in this dairyland of all Europe, that only small children had a ration. The Germans had taken ninety per cent of the dairy herds away to Germany, so the loss of one cow was felt by the whole small community.

There was a gentle knock on the door and in came the old man with a trayful of wonderful-looking macaroni, mashed potatoes and apple pie, in quantities normally sufficient to feed ten men. It all went down, to his surprise, while he talked in a hushed whisper of everything he had done that morning. He said he had to keep quiet because he was not telling his children about me because he thought they would be bound to give the show away. It was wise.

I started to ask him about the war and how far the Allies had reached. He had only the vaguest ideas, and I found this to be general with nearly all the Dutch civilians. No papers were published and their only source of news was the B.B.C. and rumour. The latter really produced some wonderful tales which included anything from additional bridgeheads across the Rhine to airborne landings near the Zuyder Zee. It was obvious that I would have to get up and find out for myself what was going on, so I asked him in my mixture of English, German and French, whether he could get me some clothes and a bicycle. He thought he could to-morrow, but to-day I must stay where I was. I could do little else, as all I had on were my underclothes, so for the rest of the day I rested.

I wondered how Evie my wife was. Poor girl, she was expecting our first child in January, and she would probably be worried sick by hearing no news. I heard later that my Colonel had told her when he arrived back on October 1st that he did not think there was much hope for me, as an eye-witness had seen a mortar bomb explode where I had been standing. With any luck, he said, I might be wounded and a prisoner of war, but she must not count on such good fortune.

Next day I felt hot and feverish, with my chest wheezing like a steam engine. I had clearly got bronchitis which no doubt was partly the result of getting so run down during the previous fortnight. For four days I felt very ill and could not eat at all. The poor old couple looked very worried, and I think the man was beginning to wonder if he had a chronic invalid on his hands. Eventually on the fifth day the fever left me and I began to feel better, but my legs seemed weaker than ever. I decided that I must get in touch with the Resistance movement and ask for some help to get back across the Rhine. Kind as the old people were, I did not feel

I was getting anywhere while I stayed with them, and I would achieve much more if I could get in with some more active members of the Resistance.

Reluctantly he agreed to go and see somebody who, he thought, could help. Everybody in Holland thought he knew who was in the Resistance and who was not. Very few really knew. I think the old man was rather proud of his "Tommy." When his best friends called on him, he would lead them up to my room and show me off like a prize cow to be prodded and discussed in a sort of detached matter-of-fact tone. When I reached safety I registered his name as a man who had given me help, and after the war he received a certificate, well-printed on vellum, to say how grateful the Allies were for his patriotism. It is his most treasured possession and hangs to-day in an honoured place in his living-room.

On the afternoon of the sixth day he came in to say that he had arranged for me to go somewhere where it was better organised for people like myself, and where there would not be so much chance of discovery. His one idea was to hide me. My one idea was to get away and back to England. My bronchitis had, however, enforced idleness upon me so I was really most grateful for all the old couple had done for me.

I quickly dressed and went downstairs, in the fading light, to meet another man who had a spare bicycle. I was to follow him at about a hundred yards distance to a new address. I took leave of the old pair, and thanked them from the bottom of my heart for all the kindness they had shown me. I will never forget them.

As we bicycled slowly along the streets, it felt quite queer to be once more on the road. I was dressed in an old dingy black pair of trousers and a blue shirt, which gave me local atmosphere. My only worry was that the Germans had an awkward habit of suddenly setting up a check-point, to round up able-bodied men for work on field defences which in this case they were building along the line of the Ijssel River. However, we avoided all check-points although we saw a lot of Germans walking or marching about. In due course we arrived at the door of a suburban semi-detached villa in the side streets of Velp. Inside I was met by my new host and hostess, Mr. and Mrs. Huisman, and their two children aged eight and five. What an incredible family! They were already sheltering two refugees. One, a Dutchman who had escaped from a concentration camp and who had to lie low, and the other a Polish-German Jew whose race made him a marked man.

My host was the local schoolmaster from the primary school, and a more jovial, God-fearing, and brave man I have never met. His wife was equally wonderful, and in a tiny two-bedroomed villa squeezed seven people, cooked for them, using many gifts of food from friends, and even managed to keep the house looking extremely clean. Potatoes were the big filler-up at meals. We refugees used to peel them and wash up. Huge soup plates full of mashed potatoes with a little meat gravy were helped down by bread smeared with a scraping of butter and sugar sprinkled on top. Before and after every meal the schoolmaster said grace, while we dutifully stood with bowed heads behind each chair, our potatoes already doled out in front of us. The graces were impromptu and lasted about ten minutes. In the evenings the Bible was always read for ten minutes after the meal, and on Sundays a hymn was sung to the schoolmaster's accompaniment on a harmonium organ he had in his living-room. Most of the Dutch families I met followed similar routines, and were usually members of the Dutch Reform Church which I believe to be strictly Calvinistic in its preachings and outlook.

A hide-out had been dug under the floor of the front room and was entered through a hatch formed from the floor boards which would be difficult to notice except during a very thorough inspection. At first we all slept in it, but I found it so dank and stuffy that I slept on the floor of the living-room just above.

Pete was my real contact with the world. I believe he was a proper member of the Resistance, although it was a question which was never asked in Holland at that time. He had light red hair and an open smiling face. He gave me the impression that he was prepared to take any risk in the service of his country and no job would be too much trouble for him. He came in on the evening of the first day, with my new host on one arm, and on the other a big basket load of eggs, butter and potatoes for the household. He told me that a Major Hibbert was over near Ede, about ten miles away, and they were able to use a telephone that communicated direct to Nijmegen, fifteen miles inside the British lines. The line was a private one which had been installed by the local electric power company. The Germans apparently did not know of its existence and never discovered it. It was used by our Intelligence Services until the end of the war, and was an ideal way of getting information through quickly.

The plan being formed to get us to the British lines was

divided into three parts. First, as many British troops as possible who were hiding up or living in the woods would be located and contacted. Then it would be necessary to concentrate them at the river at the right time and without the Germans discovering. Lastly there were the boats to get us across, together with any diversionary activities which might be laid on from the British side to distract the Germans' attention.

In the meantime everybody was to lie low and not excite too much attention, as it would take at least fourteen days to organise the whole affair. The magnitude of the problem can be understood when it is realised that more than a hundred and twenty British troops were scattered over as many square miles all round Arnhem, and all living more or less in secret. The majority had evaded capture and had been living for the previous ten days or so either off the land or thanks to the hospitality of our good Dutch friends. It would be the Resistance's task to make arrangements to gather us all together on a specified date and time a fortnight later. In the meantime, Tony Hibbert and Digby Tatham-Warter would make detailed reconnaissances in the Ede area to find a suitable concentration point near the river and a route down to it which evaded the German positions. I sent word to them asking if they wanted any assistance, but they said that the fewer in the area the better so it would be better if I stayed where I was for the time being. So all I had to do was to sit and wait. How very boring!

Pete also told me that Tony Hibbert had managed to escape by jumping off the truck which was taking them away to permanent prison camps in Germany. The German guards had lost their heads and turned their tommy-guns on to the rest of the lorry load killing two and wounding three more. Tony had jumped off in the middle of a Dutch town nearby, and had soon shaken off two Germans who ran after him.

At that moment a refugee Dutchman came running in to say that a German patrol was approaching, so we had better get down into our hideout in case they came in. Quickly we clambered down and one of the children shut the trap-door on top and smoothed over the carpet. All we could hear was our own heavy breathing and an occasional footstep in the room above. The atmosphere was tense and all of us wondered whether the hated Germans were to come to our house or pass on to some other unfortunate people. Always hiding, hiding, hiding.

Someone came over to our trap-door and gave us the signal to open up. The patrol had passed and we could all have supper. Mrs. Huisman already had the frying pan out and was making pancakes which were a rare delicacy in 1944 Holland. The *Pannacuchen* were lovely, the first rich food I had tasted in Holland, and soon the whole house was full of the deep aroma of frying batter. I shall never forget that smell, nor the excitement of the children when they heard what their meal was going to be. A continuous diet of potatoes and bread, sufficient though it may be, gradually produces an inner craving for something richer and more full of flavour. The *Pannacuchen* were just what we all wanted.

I was getting so out of touch with the news of the outside world that I asked if anybody had a wireless set that still worked. The trouble was that the Germans had cut the power off in all parts of the town except where their own Headquarters were located. The majority of the Dutch houses used to listen to the B.B.C., but now they could not do so because there was no electricity. On the other hand all the houses in the street where the German Divisional H.Q. was located had electricity, and so we walked round there to a friend, who let us listen to his wireless. It was wonderful to hear the calm voice of the announcer giving out the news; it inspired us with a renewed confidence. No wonder the Germans tried to stop it. There were a lot of Germans around the H.Q., of course, but they took no notice of us, and afterwards I often went round in the evening to keep up to date.

One day yet another British soldier came to stay in our crowded little house, a lance-corporal military policeman who had been at Divisional H.Q. The Dutch were beginning to organise the concentration of British troops and reduce the number of different places where they were in hiding. He was a nice enough chap and soon fitted into our strange household.

Chapter XVIII

RHINE CROSSING

W<small>E HAD</small> a wonderful party the night before we left. Some friends came in carrying bottles of Arak gin. Somebody else brought in a covered basket as a special present for "the poor British officer who is so thin" from a Baroness van Heemstra and her daughter. On opening up the basket, I found a bottle of vintage Krug champagne, a jar full of beef tea and some coffee. Straightaway I wrote a note of thanks to go back by hand, little knowing that my unknown admirers were living in the next-door house to where I had hid in the cupboard. I would have been even more incredulous, if someone had told me that the daughter would one day grow up into the beautiful stage and film actress Audrey Hepburn.

The delicacies that they had sent round were literally more valuable than gold in wartime Holland, and were freely given to a complete stranger. I later heard that the Heemstra family were themselves suffering terrible shortages of food and that little Audrey was even too weak to dance. Such was true generosity which I will always remember.

All the Dutch became exceedingly merry, and by the light of flickering candles they were soon singing patriotic songs in quick succession at the tops of their voices.

Thoughts of war and Germans were pressed into the background. Here, at least, was a little piece of patriotic Holland trying to forget its worries and anxieties.

An urgent tapping at the door went unnoticed at first. Somebody at last heard it, and putting up his finger said one word, "*Moffen.*" The noise stopped; the house was still once again, and smiles left every face. The word "*Moffen*" was the Dutch equivalent of our "Hun," and was a forbidden word in wartime Holland. What was the trouble now?

My host spoke through the door to the person outside and, on identification, opened the door. Apparently we had woken him up in his house about a hundred yards away, and he had come to warn us that the German billeted with him might wake up too.

By dawn next morning we were all dressed and ready to start on the final lap of our return home. A lorry, used for evacuating civilians from Arnhem, would call for us and take us to the woods near Ede, where the major concentration was taking place. A wheezing old lorry drew up at the house, and already had six civilians seated in it. Who they were I do not know, and they exhibited no surprise when we climbed in and lay on the floor under some sacks—just in case a German check-point should ask for our passes.

The lorry was driven by charcoal gas and bumped and swayed through the streets of Arnhem and down the main road to Ede. From my place, on the floor, I could see the sky and trees overhanging the road and the second floors of houses as they went by. I began to feel an elation that I had not had for weeks. At last we were on the move again! I had a feeling of overwhelming gratitude to the good Dutch people for sheltering us and now getting us away.

For their part, they were glad to have the opportunity of taking an active part in the war to help their country. But I was, nevertheless, exceedingly grateful for all they had done for us.

Through a crack in the side of the lorry I could see burnt-out German lorries which had been caught by the ever-watchful R.A.F. Typhoons with their rockets. Every German in the area had one eye in the sky and the other on the road. Every car or lorry had an air-warning sentry sitting on the front mudguard, looking backwards and upwards. Even then the R.A.F. occasionally surprised German convoys on the road before the sentries could shout their warnings, and awful bloody havoc and ruin resulted.

We were now on the road between Arnhem and Ede and the forest was nearly continuous on either side, except for an occasional white-fronted house set back in the trees. The lorry suddenly stopped and the passenger who had been sitting next to the driver jumped out and signalled us to follow suit. Nobody else was in sight and we had soon walked down a footpath leading into the forest, with the noise of the old lorry getting fainter as it continued on its way to Ede.

After twenty minutes' walk we came to a small clearing with a tiny hut in the middle. To my astonishment it was surrounded by about thirty British soldiers who were busying themselves in small groups all round. Some were sorting equipment, others cooking up some hot water, while nearly all were exchanging tales of their wanderings. Inside the hut, which was built as a shooting lodge, were crowded another twenty men or so, and a high old stench of unwashed bodies wafted out of the door as we looked in.

Tony Hibbert suddenly saw me and let out a cheer which was taken up by all around. I suppose the others had thought we were Dutchmen, dressed as we were, in very nondescript civilian clothes. I remember I had an incredibly battered old felt hat that had seen many seasons during its lifetime, and was more suitable for a scarecrow.

It was wonderful to hear up-to-date news again and to feel that we were at last getting somewhere. Two brigadiers were hiding in Ede, one being Brigadier Hackett who commanded 4th Parachute Brigade which had come in on the second day. The dropping zone was under small-arms fire when the Brigade landed, but in spite of this they succeeded in rallying the battalions to take part in the battle round Divisional H.Q. later on in the operation. The Brigadier was hit at close range by a machine-gun burst and was made a prisoner. Some of our own surgeons operated on him in a nearby German hospital which was mostly full of British soldiers, and a day later the Dutch Resistance took him out on a stretcher under the very eyes of the German guards. He was now rapidly recovering in a Dutch house in Ede.

Brigadier Lathbury had been wounded whilst trying to get to his H.Q. on the bridge and had been taken into the same hospital as Brigadier Hackett. After a few days he saw his chance and hobbled off to spend the next ten days living in the woods to the north of Arnhem, eventually finding refuge in another house near Ede.

My only trouble was my shoes. My boots had been too obviously British and I had left them with my policeman friend in Velp. The shoes I had on were horribly uncomfortable and sharply-pointed with thin businessman's soles. Pat

Glover, the quartermaster, soon fixed me up with a pair of boots he had scrounged off a dead British soldier. Pat had foreseen our requirements and had been collecting boots and smocks from British dead for the last few days.

The hut was one of two collection areas, the other being much nearer to our river crossing. Our area was about ten miles from the river, but the other was only about three miles from it. The plan was to concentrate everybody at the nearer one and we could move there by lorry at nightfall and then the whole party would be guided down to the crossing point. Digby Tatham-Warter had carried out a brilliant reconnaisance the night before and had mapped out a route that led down to the river, avoiding all German troop positions. Without Digby's reconnaissance the whole plan would have failed.

By four o'clock everbody was sorted out into small groups and the whole area had been scavenged for incriminating evidence. The Dutch were to lay on the lorries, and we were to be hidden in the undergrowth fifty yards from the edge of the main road by ten minutes to six.

Slowly the minutes dragged by to zero hour and the start of our last lap. Our only immediate worry was the possibility of an inquisitive German patrol finding us, but, unless they had information of our whereabouts, this was most unlikely. The only thing that worried me was the enormous size of our party. However quiet each one might try to be, a hundred and twenty men moving through woods at night would sound like an army.

I was half asleep when a low whistle woke me, and we were on our way to the roadside. At six sharp, three old covered lorries rattled down the road, and drew up opposite us with a squeal of brakes. The fifty of us piled in quickly and lay on the floor, while the Dutch drivers covered us with empty sacks, so that we looked like lorries full of potatoes. If a German check-point should stop us, which would be most unlikely, we would try and bluff it. If that failed we would have to jump out and overpower the post.

We were soon bumping on our way and after twenty minutes or so passed through Ede, which was being used as an H.Q. for the Division defending the sector of the river where we were to cross. It was now nearly dusk, and two German check-points waved us through without stopping us. We were obviously the rations convoy going up to the regiments on the river.

After another twenty minutes or so of most uncomfortable travelling, the lorries drew up at the side of the road and we all quickly jumped out. It was now nearly dark, and we filed off down a footpath. For ten minutes we stumbled over tree trunks and brambles till we came to open area where we met the rest. Gerald Lathbury and Digby were there, and dozens of others. The whole party was now a hundred and twenty strong.

Everybody was cheerful, although we all knew that the most difficult part of the operation was still ahead. We would wait till the moon rose at 9 p.m. before we started, and that would give us four hours to cover the three miles to the crossing point which we were due to reach at 1 a.m. Gerald Lathbury had spoken by telephone to the British Corps H.Q. on the other side of the river, and they were laying on the boats to get us across. They had also arranged some diversionary patrols and harassing fire to keep the Germans' attention away from our crossing point. To help us find the right place a Bofors anti-aircraft gun would fire a burst of tracer at a low angle exactly over the crossing point every thirty minutes from after midnight.

We had about an hour and a half to wait, and, knowing that I would need all my energies later on, I quickly curled up in some leaves for a sleep. All the more experienced amongst us did likewise, although the younger ones were obviously so overcome with excitement that sleep was the last thing they wanted. At 9 p.m. the moon rose and we were on our way through the forest. Where possible we would go in pairs to reduce the length of the column, but sometimes the footpath was so narrow that we had to go in single file. All we asked each man to do was to keep in sight of the one in front, and to be as quiet as possible. The Dutch were providing guides for the first two miles or so, and they were invaluable as this was the densest part of the forest.

Sometimes the trees closed in over us like a tunnel, and the moonlight was completely shut off except for an occasional shaft of light that had somehow penetrated the branches. The only noise in the forest came from wild animals; rabbits and an occasional deer could be heard running off as the noise of our approach broadcast a warning. The first time we heard a deer, everybody stopped and listened. We thought we had bumped a German post.

By 11 p.m. we had reached the edge of the forest, and about a mile of open fields now lay between us and the edge of the river. We wrung the hands of our brave Dutch guides and thanked them from the bottom of our hearts. One of them insisted on coming along with us and eventually he joined the Dutch forces then helping to liberate Holland. We had to pass between two German positions

spaced about half a mile apart, each containing a Nebel-
werfer mortar battery and some infantry. The mortars had
been firing fitfully all night, and as we came closer the ear-
splitting, tearing noise of these heavy mortars seemed to cut
into the still night air and remind us that caution was still
vital for success.

A four-foot-deep drainage ditch ran along our route. We
were able to use it as cover and bending ourselves double
we half-crawled and half-walked down its length. After an
hour we had covered about half a mile and were about level
with the German positions. Half a mile farther on we could
see the line of the river, and just at that moment a burst of
Bofors tracer came over and showed us that we were heading exactly right. It was midnight, and one hour was left to
us to get to the crossing point.

More careful crawling using the best cover we could
find, either from hedges or drainage ditches, brought us to
a road, where we could see the Germans had dug slit
trenches in the bank. Digby passed the word round that the
Germans had a standing patrol in this area the night before, so we must be as quiet and alert as possible. After a
quarter of an hour in which we all crawled up as close as
possible, there seemed to be no Germans in the position,
so we quickly ran across the road and jumped down the
bank on the far side. The river was now only two or three
hundred yards away, and we followed the line of a main
drainage ditch down to its bank.

Nothing stirred on the river save the gurgle of flowing
water, and a subdued swish from a nearby weir. A few
marsh birds occasionally let out their plaintive cries, and it
was difficult to believe that the river was no-man's-land be-

tween Germans and Allies.

We could now see the other side through a layer of swirling mist that clung to the surface of the river. No sign of life or movement could be seen anywhere. Some of the men began to talk quite loudly as we walked down the bank to our crossing point a few hundred yards farther down. Somebody hissed, and a moment later a burst of German automatic fire sounded only fifty yards away. We all went flat on our tummies with the ear-shattering noise still ringing in our ears. Were we to be cheated of success at this stage? Would we have to swim for it? A thousand doubts went through my head as I wormed forward to see what was going on. Luckily nobody was hit, and we could hear sounds of a small German patrol withdrawing hurriedly back across the fields. The Germans must have been even more frightened than we were.

We reached the chosen point and gave a pre-arranged light signal. Five, ten, fifteen minutes went by and nothing happened, except for the occasional weird, tearing screech of a German heavy mortar passing overhead. Our imagination conjured up a hundred and one things that might have gone wrong, but at last the rythmical splash of paddles could be heard, and a moment or two later three or four assault boats nosed upstream towards us out of the mist. The swift current in the centre of the river had carried them off course as they came across.

The boats were manned by sappers from 43rd Infantry Division, and three trips were needed to get us all back. This was my fourth Rhine crossing in six weeks. I had flown over it, I had swum it, I had been driven over it as a prisoner, and now I was carried across it in a boat. I preferred the last method, although I did not regret the first.

As soon as the boats grounded on the far side we leapt out and, guided by a white tape, walked half a mile to a small farmhouse, where tea and buns had been provided. Everybody was now laughing and talking about what they would do when we arrived back in England, and in a carefree way we piled aboard some waiting transport that was hardly big enough for our large party. Tony Hibbert and I jumped on to a jeep that already had five others in it, and Tony had to sit on the bonnet in front. The driver had come from Corps H.Q. and he had never been so near the front line before, and his one idea was to get back as quickly as possible. Off we drove at twenty miles an hour, without lights, and went straight into the back of a lorry in front. Tony bore the full force of the crash on his legs, which were broken in two places. It was incredibly bad luck and we all felt very sorry for him. It was many months before he was able to leave hospital, and he will always have a slight limp.

At 3 a.m. on October 23rd we arrived at the Corps Casualty Clearing Station established in a school near Nijmegen and there we spent the rest of the night. Next day we were thoroughly questioned and I was able to pinpoint the German Divisional H.Q. in Arnhem for the benefit of some future air attack and also pass on the names of all those good Dutchmen who had helped me in the previous two and a half weeks.

After another night in the C.C.S. we were driven twenty miles to an airfield where six American C47s waited to fly us back to England.

At 2 p.m. we landed at the same Lincolnshire airfield

from which I had taken off some six weeks previously. Near the control tower I could see a few cars waiting and I spotted one from my unit.

"Sergeant-major sent me, sir."

"Did you know I was coming?"

"Well, not exactly, sir. We heard that a party had got back from across the Rhine and the sergeant-major said you was a dead snip to be with it. I think he has had a bet, you see, sir."

THE END

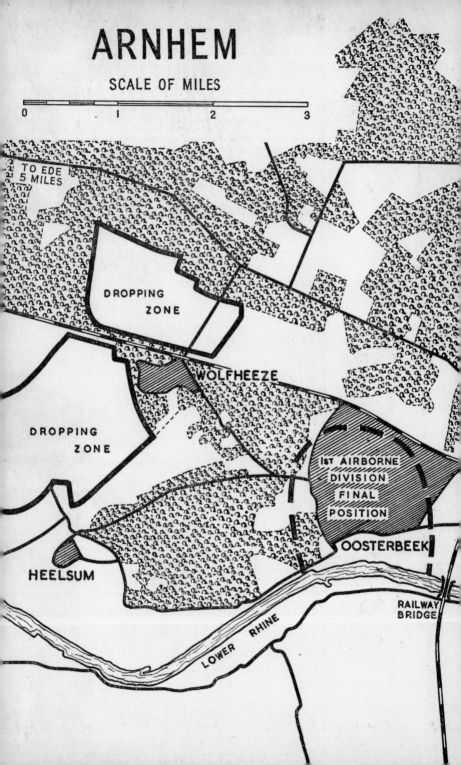